The Wonderful Ride

THE WONDERFUL RIDE

Being the true journal of Mr. George T. Loher who in 1895 cycled from coast to coast on his Yellow Fellow Wheel

With commentary by his grandaughter, Ellen Smith

A WESTWORD Book

Published in San Francisco by
HARPER & ROW, PUBLISHERS
New York, Hagerstown, San Francisco, London

THE WONDERFUL RIDE
Being the True Journal of Mr. George T. Loher
Who in 1895 Cycled from Coast to Coast On
His Yellow Fellow Wheel.

FIRST EDITION
Designed by Patricia Brunning

Library of Congress Cataloging in Publication Data

Loher, George T.
  The wonderful ride.

  "A Westword book."
  1. Loher, George T. 2. Cyclists — United States —
Biography. 3. United States — Description and travel —
1960-   I. Title.
GV1051.L63A38   1978   796.6 [B]   78-3358
ISBN 0-06-250540-8

Portland
★

Billings
★

San Francisco
★

Contents

Minneapolis

Milwaukee

Rochester

New York

As I Remember Grandfather...

It's been more than thirty years since Grandfather Loher died, but only in the last two have I come to know him. Even now, I wonder if I really do.

Oh, I saw him often enough as a child—he lived less than an hour away. But Grandpa wasn't an easy man to know, especially for a little girl. I was only eleven when he died, and only three when he lost the one great joy of his life, my grandmother.

Grandfather was a quiet, even a gentle person, but one to be reckoned with. A wink, or more often a frown, said enough. Remembering him now, I still feel a certain awe.

Actually, he wasn't a big man—only five foot seven—but he had a broad frame that was strong even into his seventies. His hands, large and callused, never stopped working, if only to twiddle his thumbs or twirl the ends of his bushy gray mustache. His dress always seemed the same—a black suit, a black fedora, and a gold watch chain draped across his vest. I liked to watch its links sparkle in the sunlight.

Perhaps Grandpa really wants to be friendly, I would tell myself, and just can't let go. He was such a proud man, stubborn and not very diplomatic, scrupulously honest with a puritan heritage that let him find satisfaction in hard work. But there was no fun, no imagination, no adventure in him—or so I thought. I know now how wrong I was!

Grandfather had been gone for a quarter of a century, and I had grown up, married, and had five children of my own by that day in 1969 when I learned of the wonderful ride.

THE ACME CYCLIST BACK.

George Loher, Who Went From
Oakland to New York on
His Wheel.

He Encountered Much That Was Romantic, but Much More That Was
Very Unpleasant.

OAKLAND OFFICE SAN FRANCISCO CALL,
908 Broadway, Dec. 15.

Much interest was shown to-day at the
Acme Club over the tour of George Loher,
who arrived home yesterday from New
York, to which city he went on his wheel.
Loher's trip was one of the most arduous
and difficult ever undertaken. Instead of
riding from ocean to ocean by the most
direct and accessible route, as all previous
cross-continent riders have done—with the
exception of Tom Winder—Mr. Loher pre-
ferred to take his way over some of the
wilde-t and roughest portions of the country. He left Oakland on August 11 in
company with a friend named Cornell, but
his companion turned about at Sacramento
and came home.

Loher skirted the Pacific Coast to Portland, and then made his way East through
Idaho, Montana, the Dakotas and Minnesota, to Chicago, from which point he followed the beaten track of travel to New
York, where he arrived by October 30.

The trip was not taken with any view of
crossing the continent on record time, but
nevertheless Loher's time over the most
difficult portion of the route—that west of

GEORGE T. LOHER OF THE ACME CLUB, WHO RODE TO
NEW YORK FROM OAKLAND ON A WHEEL.

*I was looking through a box of mother's old photo-
graphs and came upon a yellowed clipping from the long-
defunct San Francisco Call, datelined December 15,
1895. It carried a sketch of a young man with a handlebar
mustache standing beside a bicycle, and next to it was a
news story headlined: "THE ACME CYCLIST BACK.
George Loher, Who Went From Oakland to New York on
His Wheel." Grandfather?*

*Yes, Mother said, it was he. In fact, he had written
an account of the trip shortly after he got back—Uncle
George still had it. She seemed surprised that somehow, in
all the years I was growing up, no one had ever bothered to
mention Grandfather's amazing trip. But then, Grandfather himself never mentioned it. It was just something he
had done, long ago; it was over, so why talk about it?*

Then she sat down and told me the story.

Grandfather was a young man at the time, twenty-nine, single, and working at Fred Becker's Central Market in Oakland. The young butchers there had some merry times together, and apparently Grandfather was one of the leading cutups. At least, on the occasion of one evening's picnic at Trestle Glen (then a popular spot east of Lake Merritt), he is said to have clambered up onto a parked locomotive, put a match to its lantern for light, then proceeded to dance several young ladies around the grassy floor. The event was commemorated in a long doggerel epic that I found among the photographs.

Cycling was the craze of the day, and some of the boys at Becker's became enthusiastic wheelers. They joined the Acme Cycling Club and enjoyed outings and competition with other local groups. But there was a big world out there beyond the Bay Area, and Grandfather and Thomas Cornell, another butcher at Becker's, decided that they should see it—on wheels.

They would pedal from Oakland to Portland, then across the continent to New York. Grandfather insisted that they were not out to set any records, so one can only wonder about the unusual route. Most cross-country cyclists rode directly between San Francisco and New York, a much shorter and less rigorous trip. They also chose to travel without maps—a decision Grandfather would soon regret.

On August 11, 1895, the two young butchers rode out of Oakland on their grand excursion, accompanied to the outskirts by a farewell contingent of "Acme boys." Cornell was destined to return in a few days, but for George T. Loher it was the start of a grueling eighty-day adventure that would end at the foot of Manhattan Island.

Grandfather must have kept a diary faithfully, for the name of virtually every town, river, hotel, and person he encountered found a place in his journal. Sad to say, those notes and the longhand draft he wrote promptly upon his return to Oakland have all vanished. But a typed copy has remained in the family and forms the basis for this book.

So far as I know, no part of the journal has ever seen print. My mother recalls that many years later, in 1928, two men came to his shop one day to talk to Grandfather about publishing it, but he flatly refused. In fact, he was downright irritated that they should even suggest such a thing. Why, I don't know. His reaction is hard to understand, but then so was Grandfather.

Naturally, the journal has a lot of personal meaning for me. But from the first time I read it, I've felt that people outside the family might enjoy it, too, and I've dreamed of seeing it published. Slowly, I began to track down missing bits of information and answers to questions the journal raised. Then, in the spring of 1976, I met Patricia Kollings of Westword Associates, who shared my enthusiasm for the project. With her editorial guidance, my efforts gained momentum, and together we have developed this book. So far, everyone involved with the project has found great delight in it. We hope the reader will, too.

We have altered Grandfather's original text only in minor ways—omitting lists of small settlements passed through and a few routine remarks about meals or road conditions, rephrasing an occasional passage for the sake of clarity, and correcting misspellings where possible. In case of doubt, however, we've let Grandfather have his way with the spelling, no matter how questionable.

We've resisted the temptation to delete or soften any of his comments out of fear that they might sound prejudiced. After all, Grandfather was a man who had opinions on everything and expressed them frankly. We hope the reader will remember that these are statements from another era, made by a young man suddenly confronted with a wide assortment of people and cultures that were strange to him. Grandfather himself might see things quite differently now.

Anyone undertaking an adventure like this today would no doubt record his experiences on film, but the cameras of 1895 were hardly pocket models, and a cyclist had to keep weight to a minimum. Nor was Mother's box of photographs much help; it didn't contain a single snapshot of Grandfather during those years. There was the wedding portrait from the following year, and another taken several years earlier—nothing more. Eventually, I happened upon the crucial picture of Grandfather and his wheel in an 1895 issue of the old Bearings *magazine, and Louis Stein of Oakland, an authority of transportation history, located a photo of the Acme boys in his own collection.*

Lacking original photographs of the trip itself, I have tried to reconstruct the America Grandfather saw with appropriate pictures from historical societies, libraries, newspapers, and individuals along his route. In the process I have also learned a lot of interesting, often amusing sidelights that have made the journal even more enjoyable for me. To share these with the reader, I have added personal comments here and there, printed in the same italic type as this introduction.

As the journal goes to press, I'd like to say one last, private word. Thanks, Grandfather, for taking us on this wonderful ride through an America we'll never know. And thanks for letting me get to know you through your journal as I couldn't face to face. I hope you won't be upset by our publishing it now that you've gone. We just want the world to know what a determined butcher boy from Oakland could do when he set his mind to it.

Ellen Smith
April 1978

The following year Grandfather married and settled down.

Acknowledgements

*The heart of this book — both the actual adventure and the
journal — was the accomplishment of one man, Grandfather. But
the photographs and background information that embellish it
have been assembled through the interest and generosity of
many people all across the country, far more than I can possibly
acknowledge here.*

*State and local historical societies, museums, libraries, and
newspapers all along Grandfather's route have been helpful.
So have many other organizations and individuals. Some are
named in my comments or the photographic credits, but others
are not; there simply was not space to include all the marvelous
pictures and lore that they provided.*

*Among the unnamed individuals, I am especially grateful
to: Ruth Axe; A. Richard Brown, Jr.; Barry Combs, of the Union
Pacific Railroad; Marion Gerling, of the Wheelmen; Randall A.
Johnson; Mickey Karpas, of the Oakland Museum; George Kraus
and William Phelps, of the Southern Pacific Transportation
Company; Irving A. Leonard; Annette McNair, of the Alameda
County Library System; James Miller, of the Chicago Public
Library; Andrew Ritchie; Vaughn Rockafellow; J. Ronald
Shumate, of the Association of American Railroads; and
Gretchen Tyler.*

*To these people and to all the others who shared their
knowledge, resources, enthusiasm, and encouragement, my
warmest thanks.*

Chapter opening page photo credits:

Chapter 1 — "Fair Oakland" in the Nineties. (Photo courtesy: Oakland Public Library). Chapter 2 — The station at Ashland, 1886. (Photo courtesy: Southern Pacific Collection.) Chapter 3 — The locks at Cascade, Oregon. (Photo courtesy: Union Pacific Railroad Museum Collection.) Chapter 4 — The mainline of the OR&N, ca. 1890. (Photo courtesy: Union Pacific Railroad Museum Collection.) Chapter 5 — Fort Missoula, Montana, 1886. (Photo courtesy: Montana Historical Society.) Chapter 6 — Main Street, Billings, ca. 1895. (Photo courtesy: Montana Historical Society.) Chapter 7 — Sauk Center, Minnesota, 1892. (Photo courtesy: Minnesota Historical Society.) Chapter 8 — "Enterprising" Minneapolis, 1895. (Photo courtesy: Minnesota Historical Society.) Chapter 9 — A Wisconsin cyclist, ca. 1900. (Photo courtesy: State Historical Society of Wisconsin.) Chapter 10 — The Erie Canal and towpath. (Photo courtesy: Old Brutus Historical Society.)

A rather unusual notion . . . Plans and preparations . . . Farewell to the Acme boys . . . Dust, heat, and numerous head-dunkings . . . Calamity on Boehmer Hill . . . Falls in the dark . . . A tour of "The Floury City"

1

In the latter part of July, 1895, I conceived the notion of riding a bicycle across the continent, from ocean to ocean, to visit the great and "wicked" city of New York.

I was a member of the Acme Cycling Club of Oakland, California, and not caring to undertake the journey alone, found a companion in the person of Thomas F. Cornell, also a member of the Acmes and an ardent bicycle rider. We had never seen Broadway or the Tammany Tiger, and our hearts yearned to behold these things. We set about making arrangements immediately, choosing a route via Portland and Spokane Falls, through the Badlands, down Wisconsin's sandy valleys to Chicago, and then over the well-beaten paths to New York.

An agent of the American Dunlop Tire Co., with whom I had become acquainted through the Acmes, offered to supply the newly developed pneumatic tires for our trip in return for an accounting of their stability.

Our baggage consisted of a leather boot [*or saddlebag*] strapped to the frame, a roll of blankets strapped to the handlebars, and a suit of clothes strapped under the seat, the whole weighing thirty pounds.

It was the eleventh of August when we bid our friends and San Francisco good-bye. As we rode out on the San Leandro Road that beautiful Sunday morning accompanied by a number of the Acme boys, little I thought of the long, lonesome journey of hardships and vexations I was undertaking.

On reaching San Leandro, our escort bid us good-bye, and we proceeded to Castro Valley Junction. There we were met by another party of friends, but our stay was of short duration; it was nearly noon, and we wanted to reach Livermore, some thirty-six miles distant, before night.

We kept along what is called the Castro Valley Road, passing only a few roadhouses before reaching Dublin. The roads between Castro Valley Junction and Dublin are exceedingly hilly, and at that time we were compelled to wade through eight inches of dust. My companion was continually bathing his head in the numerous creeks along the road.

> *John Cronin, who lives today on Dublin Road, tells me the dust used to be at least twelve inches thick on the road. I am indebted to him for this story, which has been told in the neighborhood for years: It seems that a man was riding along the road from Dublin to Castro Valley when he spied a hat lying in the road. It appeared to be nearly new, so he dismounted to pick it up. But just as he reached for it, a muffled voice called out from under the hat, "Hey, I'm wearing this hat — and I'm on horseback!"*

On reaching Boehmer Hill, he concluded he could ride down faster than he could walk. The consequence was a broken pedal and a good shaking up, which had a tendency towards discouraging him. We were afterward told that he was not the only unfortunate who had fallen down the hill and that a great many had broken their limbs.

We were thirteen miles from Livermore at the time of this calamity, with the roads a little better than the ones we had previously come over. My companion managed to get along in very good shape, notwithstanding the disabled condition of his wheel, until he met a farmer who gave him a ride to Pleasanton, where he took the train for Livermore.

I continued on my wheel, reaching the latter place an hour ahead of him and registering at the Livermore Hotel. We succeeded in having the pedal repaired the following morning and left Livermore for Stockton at noon.

Monday
Aug. 12

The Acme boys—alas, without identifications. But that fellow in the front row center, the one wearing the captain's epaulets, does look familiar.

Photo courtesy: Louis L. Stein, Jr.

Mr. Cornell was gaining some courage now, and I was in hopes that we would proceed without further interruption. The roads from Livermore to Bethany were excellent, and with a favorable wind we made very good time.

After leaving Bethany we came onto what is called the Levee Road, eighteen miles east of Stockton. This road was an exceedingly dusty and sandy one, which completely exhausted my companion. The weather being warm made matters worse.

We rested along the road at intervals until we crossed the San Joaquin River and ran into the lowlands. Now we were worse off than ever, and my companion was completely exhausted. The only thing I could do was to sit down and wait until he regained his strength.

We then tried other tactics, such as climbing up the railroad track, but it was of no use. It would be impossible for us to drag our heavily laden wheels over the unballasted railroad ties. So we were compelled to take to the road and do the best we could until we reached Lathrop, where we had supper.

It was seven o'clock and nearly sundown when we had rested sufficiently to proceed to Stockton, ten miles distant. We were told to keep along the railroad track, there being a path along the side of the ties worn smooth by the continuous walking of traps [*sic*] between Lathrop and Stockton. We managed to get along pretty well until after nightfall; then the picnic began.

The path being narrow and the soil of a black color made it difficult to see. Consequently we had the terrifying experience of falling over the bank a number of times. But we struggled along and managed to reach Stockton without further inconvenience at half past eight, registering at

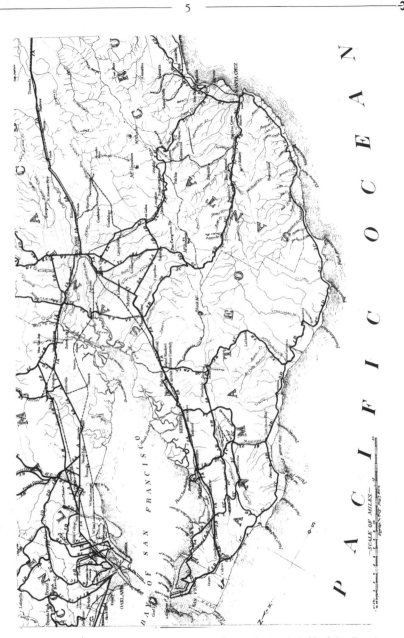

Not every wheelman chose to travel without a map. This one, showing the Oakland–San Francisco area, appeared in the Cyclists' Roadbook of California, *1893.*

Photo courtesy: Orradre Library, University of Santa Clara.

the United States Hotel.

We soon retired, for we were completely tired out after our forty-two-mile ride through the San Joaquin Valley sand.

An advertisement in the Stockton City Directory some years before Grandfather passed through (1879) described the hotel's accommodations: "This hotel and Restaurant is new and neatly furnish throughout. The rooms are airy and well ventilated. The Proprietors will use their utmost endeavors to make their Hotel an agreeable and comfortable home to those who may favor them with their patronage. —The Hotel is Open all Night. —Persons called at any hour designated, in time for the stages and cars."

Tuesday Aug. 13 The next morning found us up bright and early in order to take a walk around Stockton. Stockton is one of California's most thriving cities and has excellent shipping facilities, either by rail or water, to San Francisco. The San Joaquin River is navigable as far as Stockton, and tons of flour from the many mills along its banks are shipped daily to the metropolis. The San Joaquin–San Francisco Railroad, which is now being built, will have its terminus at Stockton. After spending the entire forenoon viewing the many beautiful things around the floury city, we returned to the hotel and made ready to leave immediately after dinner.

Sometime during their stay in Stockton, Grandfather and his friend Cornell also found time to talk to the press. The Evening Mail, *which had run a paragraph on August 12 reporting their departure from Oakland, followed up the next afternoon with a short item about their arrival in Stockton. That same day the*

rival Independent *devoted nearly ten inches to an in-
terview with the two "Oakland Boys," as its headline
called them. The latter article, which came to light last
year while I was tracking down background material
for this book, was the first inkling that anyone in the
family had ever had that Grandfather had originally
planned to go around the world. It said:*

*"They will go from here to Sacramento and thence
. . . northward into Oregon and to Portland and
Seattle. Thence they will go eastward by way of
Minneapolis to New York, where they will take the
steamer for England.*

*"They do not expect to reach the other side of the
water this year, but will winter in some Eastern city
and will earn enough to pay part of their expenses on
the other side. They selected the northern route, preferring the hard wheeling over the mountains to the
harder trip across the desert of Arizona. They expect to
reach New York by the 1st of November.*

*"They intend varying the ordinary tourist route
somewhat, for beside visiting Paris, Rome, Brussels,
Madrid, St. Petersburg and other notable places, they
will go to Egypt, the Holy land, Persia, Asia minor,
up through Russia and down through Tartary and
China. Much time will be spent in the latter country
in going over the battlefields in the late Japo-Chinese
war. They will visit Corea, Vladivostock and Eastern
Siberia."*

*Whether they had really intended such an ambi-
tious tour and Grandfather changed his mind when
Cornell deserted him, or whether they were simply
carried away by the heady experience of being interviewed, we'll probably never know. Perhaps they were*

simply misquoted —the discrepancies between various interviews along the way certainly raise that possibility. For instance, the Spokane Chronicle *said flatly, "He will not return again to San Francisco but will make his future home in New York." The nostalgia for Oakland that crept into his journal when the going got rough certainly gives the lie to that statement.*

It is understandable that Grandfather grew increasingly irritated with newspaper reporters as the trip progressed.

Mr. O. H. Schmeider, a local wheelman, kindly gave us his service as a guide out of the city. On our way out, we visited the insane asylum located on the outskirts of town, and we saw a deal of misery within its walls. One poor fellow pleaded with me to try and get his release, saying that he had been put there by designing relatives. We were glad to get out of the grounds, for from our appearances we could rightly be taken for candidates.

Mr. Schmeider then showed us to the Sacramento road and returned to Stockton. As we proceeded along on excellent roads, my thoughts returned to that poor fellow I'd left in such misery and I wondered if I could have helped him.

My thoughts were broken after we had gone only a short distance when my companion complained about his burning head, caused from the intense heat that usually prevails during the summer months through the San Joaquin and Sacramento valleys. The heat necessitated his cooling his head at a roadside watering tank.

On an average August day, temperatures will reach 90° F. around Stockton, compared to 72° in Oakland.

He decided then and there to return to Oakland upon reaching Sacramento, having concluded that he was not equal to the hardships he would have to encounter on the journey he had undertaken. I sympathized and told him he would be all right in a day or two. But it was no use giving him blarney; he was not built that way.

We sat in the cool shade of the tank and talked for some time before resuming our journey. But even so, we were unable to go far, owing to the numerous head-bathing operations that had to be gone through—much to my disgust, as I wanted to reach Sacramento that night.

We reached Lodi, one of the prettiest little towns in California, in time for supper and had the pleasure of meeting and talking with Mr. Lillie, the gentleman who had held the transcontinental bicycle record for years.

Lillie, who with his brothers operated a bicycle shop in Lodi, captured the cross-country record in 1891. One unsuccessful challenger was Frank Beedleson, who rode from San Francisco to New York in 66 days, considerably longer than Lillie's 59 days or even Grandfather's 63 days of actual ocean-to-ocean riding time. All the same, it was a rather remarkable feat— Mr. Beedleson had only one leg! Most record-seekers chose the short route across the middle of the country, but there were a few other independent souls like Grandfather. One, Tom Winder, rode around the borders of the country rather than across it, covering some 21,000 miles in 274 days, an average of more than 75 miles a day.

Then we rode on in the direction of Galt, where we were to stop for the night. When we arrived there, however, we concluded to keep riding and camp out, in order to make up time lost during the day.

We rode until nine o'clock and then, lifting our wheels over a fence, we walked to a straw stack and rolled in for the night after having traveled only twenty-five miles that day. We enjoyed the outdoor air immensely. The day had been exceedingly warm, and as the cool evening breeze fanned our heated brows, life seemed worth living after all.

Wednesday
Aug. 14 We were up the next morning before sunrise and proceeded to Elk Grove, thirteen miles distant, where we had a breakfast that would have made a dyspeptic envious. By eight o'clock we were off for our sixteen-mile ride to Sacramento over the best of roads.

We were beginning to enjoy the trip, and I was in hopes that my companion would change his mind and continue the journey, but I was sadly disappointed.

We rode to within five miles of Sacramento and stopped for a drink of water at a country blacksmith's shop. The blacksmith noticed our peculiar makeup and asked where we were going. He seemed deeply interested and told us of the hardships he had endured fighting Indians and drinking impure water while crossing the plains to California in '49. All this helped to make it utterly impossible to persuade my companion to stay. We bade the blacksmith good-bye and rode on to Sacramento, arriving there at half past ten o'clock.

The rest of the day I spent in making ready to proceed alone the following morning, while my companion packed up to return to Oakland by rail.

2 *Off on my lonely journey . . . Unexpected fire fighting . . . Wheelman's ingenuity . . . Close call with the Oregon Express . . . A chill night among the coyotes and an unplanned morning bath . . . Children, pins, and punctures*

I felt rather blue on the morning of August 15 as I arose at half past four and, bidding Cornell good-bye, rode out of Sacramento toward Woodland a little before sunrise.

Thursday Aug. 15

Sacramento was formerly my home, and as I rode down the principal street, recollections of my boyhood days came to my mind. I only wished I could have rehearsed them.

Grandfather was born on Minna Street in San Francisco on September 4, 1868, the son of a Pennsylvania carpenter named George Washington Lower. (For reasons we may guess, Grandfather later changed the spelling to Loher.) When he was only twelve, his father was killed in a fall from a rooftop, and the family moved to Sacramento to be closer to relatives. For the rest of his school years, he had to work most of his spare hours as a ranchhand to help support his mother, brother, and two sisters. At nineteen he left Sacramento to take up the butcher's trade in Oakland.

On turning down Second Street I remembered how often I had walked down to the depot on Sunday mornings, accompanied by my best girl, and watched the San Francisco trains come in, many a year ago. As I crossed the bridge and looked up the river, it reminded me of the days I played truant from school to go fishing. These recollections all seemed to cast a cloud over me, as I proceeded on my lonely journey on that beautiful summer morning.

Mr. Upton, a prominent racing man of Sacramento, had kindly mapped out a route for me as far as Redding via Woodland, Willows, and Red Bluff. After passing through the little town of Washington, I rode out past the Old Bryte Mill Ranch and the hop fields which are so abundant along the Sacramento River. They looked their prettiest that morning, and the air filled with their perfume reminded me of the large brewery located at Sacramento. I kept along the Levee road as far as Elkhorn and then rode across the swamp to Woodland, twenty miles from Sacramento, where I had breakfast.

At Williams, I witnessed a stubble fire with all the citizens out fighting it with wet sacks. It did not take long to extinguish it, and I proceeded on my way, reaching Willows at dark and registering at the Cowart Hotel.

Apparently Grandfather lent a hand in beating out the fire. When he described the incident to my uncle Frank one time in later years, he said that he left covered with soot and ashes, presenting quite a sight as he wheeled his way toward Willows.

I had been riding all that day through the famous Sacramento Valley, one of the longest and most fertile valleys in California. Wheat is raised there as high as forty-two bushels to the acre. It is extremely warm during the month of August but notwithstanding, I made a hundred miles over its smooth, level roads the first day of my lonely journey.

The following morning, August 16, I was away at five o'clock and proceeded over good roads until I met a farmer whose mules I scared by riding too close to them. I dismounted and patiently waited until he had quieted them, then politely asked the distance to Red Bluff. "Go to hell and find out," he replied and, whipping up his long-eared quadrupeds, left me standing on the roadside. *Friday
Aug. 16*

Farmers were not the only Americans who resented cyclists in the nineties. Horse-lovers saw the bicycle as a threat. Businessmen blamed it for a drop in sales of everything from carriages to theater tickets. Police found it a source of constant traffic problems. An ordinance in hilly San Francisco forbade anyone to ride a bicycle on the public streets "unless the feet of the person so riding or driving shall be kept on the pedals of the machine at all times while the machine is in motion—the practice of scorching or coasting being thereby inhibited." In early years bicycles were not even allowed on some of the major turnpikes. It was for the purpose of defending the individual rider and his right to cycle that the League of American Wheelmen was formed.

After dinner at Red Bluff, I had ridden on some eight or ten miles when I discovered that I was on my way to Norfolk instead of Redding. This necessitated my returning to within two miles of Red Bluff. After I was on the right road, I had to dismount several times owing to the rocky condition of the road.

I reached Redding at half past seven and, riding out of town for some distance, unrolled my blankets and turned in for the night under a large pine tree. It was rather cold, and I felt the want of a camp fire.

The next morning I was traveling along the headwaters of the Sacramento River without any roads for guides. Later I found a path along the side of the ties of the Oregon and California Railroad. The scenery along the river is magnificent, and the traveler is met with an abundance of running springs with which to quench his thirst.

I had not gone far when I fell over an embankment while trying to avoid running into a stake that had been driven into the center of my path. I would have had great difficulty in ascending had it not been for some section men who happened along. They threw me a rope, which enabled me to climb to the top, having experienced a shaking up and a slight scare.

I reached Smithson Station shortly after one o'clock and had dinner at what used to be a stage station but at present serves as a farmhouse. From there to Delta I had hard work making headway, owing to the rock ballasting between the tracks. Occasionally I would stop to watch the placer miners at work along the riverbanks and to view the beautiful scenery that surrounded me.

After reaching Delta, I pushed my wheel up a steep hill in an attempt to ride the wagon road, but I thought I was mistaken and returned to the track. I had continued for some distance, when I met an old gentleman coming in the opposite direction, who advised me to return to the road as I would avoid a number of tunnels and trestles. I did so and reached Sims, seven miles distant, shortly after eight o'clock, feeling rather sore and fatigued after my hard day's riding of fifty-three miles.

There are a number of squaw men throughout this section of the country. I applied to one of them for accommodations before reaching Sims but was refused, owing to the large number of children of which he was the proud possessor and who occupied all the available space in his little log cabin.

Sunday Aug. 18

The following day being Sunday I made a late start, not leaving Sims until nine o'clock. At Dunsmuir, fourteen miles away, I had the opportunity of testing my pedestrian accomplishments, for I had to walk up a twelve-mile grade to Sissons. From here I could see Mount Shasta in the distance, towering above the Coast Range with its majestic, snow-capped sides.

That grade at Sissons would probably have been hard pedaling indeed for Grandfather, because the Yellow Fellow Model A had only a 68-inch gear. Gerald L. Grulkey, California state captain of the Wheelmen's Association, tells me that this would fall in the mid-range of a modern ten-speed.

I made a half-circle around Black Butte, another high mountain, and reached Agourney, where I had supper with a farmer named Kellogg. Agourney is situated at the head of the pretty little Shasta Valley, through which I proceeded immediately after supper over the finest roads. I reached Gazelle at eight o'clock, stopping at the old stage station for the night.

Monday Aug. 19

The next morning, I was told to keep to every right-hand road to Montague, and in doing so, I had no difficulty. From there I rode directly north to Pokeganna, an infant lumbering town on the Klamath River.

At Coles Station, where I had a fine dinner, I was close to the northern border of my native state. A few moments after leaving there, I crossed the line into Oregon riding on the track to the foot of the Siskiyou Mountains. I had a steady climb of four miles before reaching the summit, at which point I displayed a wheelman's ingenuity by tying a quantity of brush together and trailing it through the dust. This enabled me to ride down the steep mountainsides with ease for a distance of ten miles.

Coaster brakes were not available until 1898, but Stearns bicycles could be ordered equipped with hand brakes on the front wheel. Some stout-hearted cyclists, however, felt that brakes added unnecessary weight, preferring to back-pedal, apply a well-timed shoe sole to the tire, or contrive some more ingenious device, such as Grandfather's drag of brush. My mother recalls that years later, when his children began riding bicycles, her father still considered brakes a useless appendage.

After reaching the foot I had excellent wheeling to Ashland, Oregon, where I had supper at the Ashland Hotel. It was not yet dark and I decided to continue to the next town, but darkness overtook me and I was compelled to stop for the night and unroll my blankets by the roadside. I was now in what is commonly called Rogue River Valley, which extends from Ashland to Grants Pass.

*Tuesday
Aug. 20*

The following morning, August 20, found me up and on my way to Medford, reaching there at seven o'clock. Medford is a much prettier place than Ashland and boasts of a large brewery and pork packing establishment. The

Oregon's roads were dotted with ever-hopeful families of "movers"—and its dry hillsides with the hopeless remains of the farms they left behind.

Photo courtesy: Oregon Historical Society.

hotel proprietor seemed to take great pride in telling me of the many advantages the town had over its neighbors.

It began to rain while I was eating breakfast, so I concluded to wait until it cleared up. No doubt you all know the excessive wet weather Oregon is subjected to. There is hardly a month in the year that escapes rain. This was merely a summer shower, and at half past eight it had cleared up sufficiently to allow me to proceed on my way.

I found very good riding by keeping along the Rogue River until I crossed it sixteen miles south of Grants Pass. Here I entered the foothills of the Cow Creek Mountains and again experienced miserable riding.

I had a narrow escape from death coasting down a hill a few miles north of the place where I crossed the river. Having reached the top of a small hill, and surveying it with the utmost surety, I decided to ride down but had not gone far before I lost complete control of my wheel. Flying down at a tremendous rate of speed over rocks, chuckholes, and other obstacles, I came to a turn in the road, which I failed to see owing to the dense foliage that abounds in these hills. The railroad runs along here, and I had to cross the track in making the turn. I held onto the wheel for dear life and succeeded in reaching the bottom in safety. But I had hardly brought my wheel to a stop when the Oregon Express train came thundering along at full speed. Had I been a minute later, I would certainly have been dashed to pieces.

I gave my wheel a good looking over, saw it had sustained no damage, and so proceeded on my way, feeling a little nervous after my singular experience.

I reached Grants Pass at noon and had dinner at the Blackburn Hotel. The poor, ill-fated Frank Lenz had eaten dinner at this same hotel only two years before. Everybody around the place eagerly inquired for him, but I could only give them such information as I had read in the daily papers.

Frank Lenz, then twenty-five, left Pittsburgh on May 15, 1892, to bicycle around the world, east to west. He wrote articles for Outings *magazine en route. While riding through Turkey in the spring of 1894, he disappeared. Investigators hired by the magazine and the Lenz family could learn little, but the following year information leaked back to the United States that strongly suggested Lenz had been killed. His body was never found.*

I had no maps and in order to get my bearings I had

to consult maps on the walls of the hotels as I went along. At Grants Pass a young man by the name of Parker rode out of town with me and directed me to the right road. I was now in the heart of the Cow Creek Mountains, or, as they are commonly called, Hungry Mans Gulch.

I had not gone far after my escort had left me, when I saw a little boy riding a pony and driving three hungry-looking cows. Behind him two footsore dogs were trying to keep from being run over by a covered wagon, which was loaded with household goods and driven by a young girl. A three-horse team brought up the rear, with the father, mother (with a nursing babe-in-arms), and some dozen or more children. The whole family were on the move. I saw a great number of such outfits going in either direction. They are called "movers" in Oregon.

It is surprising what a number of children Oregon produces; every farmhouse that I passed contained several. I often wondered if the government was making special inducements for their increase. It was amusing to see them run out and gaze at me with surprise as I rode by or stopped for a drink of water.

Riding was out of the question by this time, owing to the mountainous condition of the country that I was passing through. But nevertheless I managed to reach Wolf Creek, an old stage station twenty-six miles from Grants Pass, for supper. After partaking of a hearty meal I applied for accommodations for the night but was refused. This compelled me to go farther into the mountains and camp out.

The people throughout here seem to be opposed to the bicycle, blaming it for horseflesh being so cheap. I took it for granted that was the reason they refused to make room for me.

I kept on until after dark, then gathered some wood, built a camp fire, and turned in for the night.

Occasionally I would hear the screech of an owl or the bark of a coyote, which had a tendency toward making me wish for my warm bed in Oakland. After placing my revolver within easy reach, I was soon fast asleep. I had not slept long before I was awakened by the cold. My fire had burned out, and this compelled me to gather a new supply of wood in order to sleep comfortably for the rest of the night.

The next morning was cold and cloudy, making my surroundings anything but pleasant. I was up and on my way to Galesburg before daylight.

Wednesday Aug. 21

The scenery through here does not vary. There is an abundance of large pine and oak trees, and as one reaches the numerous high points and looks down into ravines below, a scene is produced that I will venture to say is truly fascinating.

Down one hill I would walk and up another. Riding was not to be thought of. I must have kept up this sort of a thing for an hour or more before coming to what is called Cow Creek, whence the mountains derive their name. There was no bridge across the creek, and I was in a quandary as to know how to ford it. I could see where the wagons forded, but I had no idea how deep it was.

Not having had my breakfast, I was hungry and decided to get across, even at the cost of a ducking. So I walked up along the bank to where I could see the rocks projecting out of the water at intervals all the way across. Picking up my wheel and placing it on my head, I started to ford the stream.

MODEL A.

All the world awheel will find no better mount for steady road work than this, a solid, graceful, light and artistic machine. The specification embraces every essential feature of the latest improvements. It furnishes a range of choice that will enable every rider to select a felicitous combination, making the wheel as personally suitable as though it had been expressly built for him. The Stearns Model A is a thoroughly well-bred wheel in that it does its work quietly and effectively; and it is particularly a wheel that may be

SPECIFICATIONS (MODEL A).—22, 24 or 26-inch frame. 28-inch wheels with flangeless tubular hubs, 28 spokes in front, 36 in rear. Stearns wood rims. 1⅝-inch Palmer tires. Stearns ¼-inch hardened chain. Stearns 6½-inch flat cranks. Stearns 3½-inch rat-trap pedals. Stearns adjustable seat-post. Stearns saddle. Stearns detachable sprocket. Stearns adjustable handle-bar No. 1-A. Orange-tipped corkaline handles. Tool-bag with Stearns rear axle step, air pump, oiler and wrench.

WEIGHT.—With rims, but without tires, 19 pounds. With 1⅝-inch Palmer tires, 22½ pounds.

FINISH.—Full orange. Nickeled spokes and fittings. Gear, 68 inches. Tread, 4¾ inches. Wheel base, 43¾ inches.

OPTIONS.—Black frame and orange rims. 60, 64, 72, 76, 80, 84 or 88 gear. 7, 7½ or 8-inch cranks. Stearns 3½, 3¾ or 4-inch rubber pedals. Stearns lamp bracket. Coasters. No. 2-A, 3-A, 4-A, 5-A or 6-A handle-bars. Stearns front wheel brake, fitted to No. 4-A handle-bar only. T seat-post.

STEARNS MODEL A.   PRICE, $100.

The Stearns Yellow Fellow Year Book *for 1896 assured wheelmen that there was "no better mount for steady road work" than Grandfather's Model A.*

What Grandfather so blithely put on his head was no featherweight modern racing bike. The frame of the Stearns Model A weighed 19 pounds and the tires 4½ pounds a pair. Add to that 30 pounds of personal gear, and you have an unwieldly 53½-pound load — a hard-headed fellow, Grandfather!

I had not gone far when I slipped on a round-edged rock and fell headlong into the water. There I was, hungry, wet, and cold, and three miles from Galesburg, where I was to get breakfast. I waded across regardless of the consequences after that, as I could get no wetter.

I reached Galesburg, an old, deserted stage station, at seven o'clock. Breakfast was over but the Chinese cook got something for me to eat, while I dried myself off near the stove.

It was some time before I had dried my clothes sufficiently to proceed, and during that time the children (this house was no exception with regard to children) were amusing themselves poking pins into my tires. On coming out of the house, I found both tires as flat as pancakes and consumed some time repairing them. These were the first punctures I had had up to this time. Thereafter I was very careful not to let my wheel out of my sight when there were children around.

The roads continued miserable to Cannonville, a small mountain town twenty miles from Galesburg, where I had dinner. There had been a dance the previous night, and I found almost all the inhabitants asleep at that late hour.

One o'clock found me leaving Cannonville for a forty-mile ride to Roseburg. I was out of the mountains by this time, with the roads somewhat better than the ones I had previously come over. I reached Roseburg at six o'clock, and registered at the Depot Hotel.

The muscles in my right leg swelled some during the night, but notwithstanding I was off the next morning at seven o'clock.

Thursday
Aug. 22

I had gone some eight or ten miles when I discovered my watch missing—I had left it under the pillow at the hotel. The roads were too rough to think of returning, so it necessitated my telegraphing and having the watch sent to Portland. My only companion was gone now, and you may rest assured I was very glad to receive it on reaching Oregon's metropolis.

The roads were beginning to be bad again and remained so as far as the head of the Willamette Valley.

The first town of any importance after leaving Roseburg is Oakland (not the fair Oakland I started from), which is the center of exportation for the many tons of hops that are raised throughout this part of Oregon.

Shortly after leaving Oakland, I came to what is called Mill Hill. This hill has a very steep grade two miles long on the south side, and a gradual descent on the north side, which I rode down with ease. The scenery over this hill is beautiful and more than repaid me for the time expended in climbing the grade.

I reached Yoncalla at noon and had dinner at the only hotel in town. I had an enormous appetite, and you may rest assured I was fed at a loss to the hotel proprietors.

I was out of the mountains once more and at the head of the Willamette Valley. The Willamette Valley extends from Cottage Grove to Oregon City, a distance of nearly a hundred miles, and is from five to twenty-five miles wide and comparatively level. But unfortunately, the roads were rocky, and a strong north wind was blowing at the time I passed through, which made riding difficult.

I intended to reach Eugene for the night, but within seven miles of there, darkness overtook me and made it impossible to continue, so I concluded to camp out. It was a beautiful night and a straw stack near at hand offered excellent accommodations.

Arising at daylight I rode to Eugene and breakfasted at the Hoffman House. Eugene is the largest and most prosperous of the several cities in the Willamette Valley. The state university is situated there. It is a pretty place, especially so at that early hour, seven o'clock, and as usual a large crowd congregated about my wheel as it stood in front of the hotel.

There are two ways to go to Albany from Eugene; one is by way of Corvallis, and the other by Harrisburg. I chose the latter route and, mounting my wheel, was away by eight o'clock. Threshing and hop picking were in full sway at that time, and it was amusing to see the hop pickers look at me in amazement as I rode by.

I reached the riverbank opposite Harrisburg at ten o'clock and had to wait for the ferry to take me across. During that time I amused myself writing notes and viewing the slowly moving current of the beautiful Willamette River.

The north wind was blowing almost a gale as I left Harrisburg for Halsey, fifteen miles distant, and I reached the latter with difficulty in time for dinner.

It was half past one before I left Halsey on my way to Albany. The wind had gained somewhat in velocity and I had a notion to stop and wait until after nightfall, when the wind generally dies down; but on second thought I concluded that I could not find my way in the dark and so went on. I crossed the Willamette by the bridge at Albany at four o'clock and reached Independence that night, stopping at the Depot Hotel.

Upon retiring I left orders to be called at four o'clock in the morning in order to get an early start, as I did not care to ride the remaining sixty miles to Portland against the wind.

The hotel proprietor had directed me to Portland via Salem and Oregon City, in which case I would have to be ferried across the river. But upon going down to the ferry, I could not find anyone to take me across at that early hour, which necessitated my riding up on the north side.

Saturday Aug. 24

According to the Oregon Historical Society, this is "a hopyard crew in Douglas County, ca. 1890." Presumably the dog worked free.

Photo courtesy: Oregon Historical Society.

As a general rule the inhabitants of small towns are late risers, and Independence is no exception. Consequently I could find no one to direct me onto the right road after being disappointed at the ferry. I returned to the hotel but found that the watchman had gone back to bed after calling me. I did not care to awaken him and so took a chance and proceeded on my way, reaching Bethel, a small settlement six miles north of Independence, at six o'clock. I applied for breakfast but was told that I would have to go to the next town, Amity, as the Bethel Hotel had ceased to exist many years ago. I did as directed and arrived at half past seven, as hungry as a bear.

From Amity to Portland, a distance of forty miles, I found the roads extremely rugged owing to the mountainous condition of the country, which made my riding anything but pleasant.

Within a few miles of Portland, I stopped at a farmhouse for a drink of water. Here a pitiful sight met my gaze as I was setting my wheel against a tree before going into the yard. Four children came running out to meet me. One of them had no feet; he was running around on bare stumps. Another one's feet were turned inward like an Indian's but in a decidedly more noticeable way. The other two were idiots and, upon coming up to where I stood, commenced to ask me foolish questions about my wheel. I drank no water at that place; the sight was more than I could bear. Jumping on my wheel, I rode off, still wondering if Oregon was really giving a bounty for the increase of its population. As I rode away, the poor unfortunates stood gazing at me in amazement.

3

The Columbia River Gorge . . . A bumpy ride and a twenty-mile walk . . . The alkali miseries . . . Chinese and Indians, salmon and sand . . . Lost in a canyon . . . My homemade handlebars . . . Web-Footers, Sand-Winkers, and a howling babe

I arrived in Portland at four o'clock and attracted a great deal of attention as I rode through the principal streets, covered with dust from head to foot. As I went into the express office for my watch, a large crowd congregated about my wheel. Some of them surmised who I was and asked me all kinds of questions, such as, "How did you find the roads?" and "Did you have many punctures?" I finally tired of answering questions and rode off to the hotel.

This was Saturday afternoon. I had been on the road exactly two weeks and had traveled eight hundred and thirty-six miles over the worst roads. I had met with no more serious accidents than the scare, the dunking, and the little inconvenience in repairing my tires after the pins had been stuck into them. But the worst was still to come.

The following day, Sunday, August 25, I amused myself by visiting the many points of interest in and around Portland, with a friend.

Sunday Aug. 25

My wheel was sadly in need of repairs, and the whole of Monday was consumed in getting it ready for the rest of my journey. In the evening I was entertained by the Portland Athletic Club and spent a most enjoyable evening at their beautiful club rooms on Third Street.

Tuesday morning found me making preparations to leave Portland. It was exactly one o'clock as I rode down Third Street and over the bridge to East Portland, accompanied by Mr. Cregg of the Wheelmen's Association. We rode out Burnside Street and passed the county hospital. Here my escort left me after showing me the right road.

I proceeded over excellent roads for ten or twelve miles, after which I entered the foothills of the Cascade Mountains and had miserable roads to Latourell, a small town twenty-five miles from Portland on the Union Pacific Railroad. Here I left the road and went up along the track, finding a very good path beside the ties for some distance.

One Columbia salmon wheel could scoop up fifteen hundred fish a day—a voracious harvest that Grandfather regarded with typical turn-of-the-century admiration.
Photo courtesy: Oregon Historical Society.

Not all the OR&N track was this well ballasted (as Grandfather so painfully learned), but there was no other road through much of the Columbia Gorge.

Photo courtesy: Union Pacific Railroad Museum Collection.

Wednesday
Aug. 28
I was traveling along the banks of the Columbia River by this time and had the beautiful Cascades on one side of me while one of the largest rivers in the world flowed silently on the other. The scenery here is beyond the pen of man to describe. The Cascades with their gigantic towering peaks and pretty little waterfalls create a scene that will ever be remembered by those fortunate enough to behold it.

Along the banks of the river can be seen many large wheels, similar to the old irrigating wheels in Southern California. Upon inquiry I was told that they were salmon wheels, and that the species of fish would soon be exterminated in that river. These wheels are so constructed that the action of the current revolves them, and as they revolve, the large nets with which they are equipped scoop

A night's lodging at some remote section house was better than no bed at all, and occasionally it proved to be downright congenial.

Photo courtesy: Union Pacific Railroad Museum Collection.

the fish up and toss them into a large tank that is built within five or six feet of the top. It is said that one wheel will average fifteen hundred fish a day.

That night, owing to the unsettled condition of the country, I was compelled to sleep out of doors. I was up bright and early the following morning and on my way to Cascades for breakfast, arriving at six o'clock. The government has expended thousands of dollars here in the last twenty-five years to build locks over the rapids in order to make the Columbia River navigable as far as The Dalles, forty-two miles east. It resembles a Chinese settlement to some extent, and the meal I partook of there was anything but inviting. *Thursday Aug. 29*

I left at seven o'clock feeling a little hungry. The path I have already mentioned was making itself scarce by this time, which circumstance compelled me to ride between the unballasted tracks, reaching Hood River in time for dinner, after having ridden only twenty-five miles.

Hood River is noted for the finely flavored peaches that it produces, some of which I had the pleasure of eating. After a short rest I proceeded up the track in the direction of The Dalles. I had not gone over three miles when I discovered that the rocks had cut my tires so badly as to make it utterly impossible for me to repair them. The only thing left for me to do was to drag my wheel over the remaining twenty miles of rocks and railroad ties to The Dalles. It was three o'clock when I started on my twenty-mile walk, which gave me an excellent opportunity to view the beautiful scenery. Combining work with pleasure, I reached The Dalles at half past ten, tired and disgusted. The hard walk had completely exhausted me, as I had to keep a good gait in order to arrive in time to send to Portland for new tires to be sent on the first train.

The Dalles is a town of some three thousand inhabitants and, I was told, was a lively mining camp in early days. There is an abundance of fruit raised in the vicinity, and when the Cascade Locks are finished, great things may be expected of this thriving little town.

My tires arrived the next evening, having been delayed a day, which gave me ample time to recover from the soreness brought on by the long walk.

Friday
Aug. 30

On Friday morning, August 30, I left The Dalles in the direction of Walla Walla. I was still keeping along the track and had commenced to come into sand. The high winds and sand are a source of annoyance to the railroad company through this section of the country. The company is compelled to employ a large force of Chinamen to keep the track clear. It also has board fences along the sides of the sand banks to protect the track from sand drifts. One has to continually keep a handkerchief tied about his neck in order to keep out flying sand.

As I traveled farther up the track, I saw a number of Wasco Indians spearing salmon, notwithstanding the fact that fishing season was closed at this time. They are experts with the spear and succeeded in catching large numbers of fish, which they split and nailed on boards to dry in the sun for winter use. They are a most dirty tribe, and their tents, which are made from old matting and carpets (the refuse of neighboring towns), are unsightly to behold.

It is an August day and Grandfather has been pedaling hard for hours through windblown sand. One can only wonder what those Indians might have said about him.

It is amusing to see these Indians move. They do not find it necessary to go to the express for two or three wagons as we do, but instead they pile their few belongings on their pony's back; cinching the load on, they jump on top, and away they go. It is surprising the amount of stuff their little ponies can carry.

At two o'clock I reached Deschutes, but decided to continue on to Rufus as, owing to the wind and sand, I had made very slow time that day.

I registered at the only hotel in town, and at the supper table I made the acquaintance of a Mr. Parrot, a flying machine crank. He explained his invention to me, and I

At times Grandfather paralleled the old Oregon Trail. These wagon ruts in Umatilla County must still have been very clear in 1895.

Photo courtesy: Oregon Historical Society.

was only wishing he had one with him, as I could have used it to very good advantage, flying over the Umatilla sand.

The next morning I left Rufus at seven o'clock. It was still a case of walking, with an occasional ride in some places, until I reached a cabin designated on the map as Quinns. It was occupied by a Mr. Cassidy, an old employee of the railroad company. I had commenced to feel pretty sick when I reached there from excessive drinking of the alkali water. I came very near abandoning my trip, for a while at least. Mr. Cassidy saw the condition I was in and, making a fire, brewed me a cup of tea. The poor old fellow was glad to see me, as travelers very seldom pass along there. The cabin was in a filthy condition, and I almost refused the hospitality but, owing to my weakened condition, had to accept it.

My new friend was a former resident of the San Francisco waterfront and wanted to know all about the O'Flahertys, the Caseys, and a host of others whom I was unacquainted with. I could give him very little information.

After a few hours' rest, I commenced to feel somewhat better and decided to resume my journey, against the wishes of my friend. On going to my wheel, I discovered my revolver missing from the scabbard that I had strapped on the side of my bag. I laughingly asked my Irish friend if he had taken it, as he had been examining the wheel while I was inside drinking the tea. Have you ever seen the expression on an Irishman's face when he is accused of something he is not guilty of? I could tell that he had not taken it and came to the conclusion that I had lost it.

I remembered seeing it in its place a few miles back and told Mr. Cassidy he might go back and find it and keep it for a keepsake. But he would not listen to such a proposition and insisted on my walking back with him. I did and found it lying alongside the track, where it had been shaken out of the scabbard.

We returned to the cabin, and with a hearty handshake I bid my benefactor good-bye. I will always remember the sad expression on that poor fellow's face as I left him with his dog, his only companion.

It was after one o'clock now, and I still had to walk. The section men advised me to go back in the hills and try the road, but acting upon the advice of Mr. Cregg of Portland, I concluded to stay along the track the rest of the day.

The railroad company employs Chinese section men along this part of the road and pays them ninety-five cents per day. The men receive only ninety cents, however, as the Chinese companies are paid five cents per day for each man.

Chinese crews had laid rails all across the West, and in eastern Oregon their sons were still keeping tracks clear as Grandfather rode by.
Photo courtesy: Union Pacific Railroad Museum Collection.

I managed to reach Arlington before night, having traveled only twenty-seven miles that day. It is needless to say that I was worn out and disgusted, and concluded to take the road from there the following morning, having had enough of bumping over railroad ties.

Arlington is a town of some four hundred inhabitants and has excellent accommodations. The proprietor of the Grand Hotel very kindly mapped a route out for me to Walla Walla via Cecils, Wells Springs, and Echo. I had provided myself with a flask of whiskey, in order to counteract the effects of the alkali water, and was feeling much better.

Sunday
Sept. 1 It was Sunday, September 1, when I bid some half-dozen people around the hotel good-bye and rode directly south for four miles, after which I pushed my wheel up a slight incline and found myself on the tablelands. These tablelands might be called the eastern foothills of the Cascade Mountains and are mostly unproductive.

After reaching the top, I rode in a southeasterly direction over good roads to Cecils, a small station on the Union Pacific Railroad. From there the roads were almost impassable until I passed Wells Springs.

I had been told at Arlington that I could procure my noonday meal at Wells Springs. Within five miles of the place, I inquired as to whether I was on the right road. On being answered in the affirmative, I rode on, expecting to see a small settlement, but I only passed an insignificant farmhouse, visible from a small hill on the road. This the settlers here have the audacity to call Wells Springs.

I did not discover the mistake I had made in passing Wells Springs, until I'd gotten lost in a canyon, some three miles east of it. The day being cloudy made it impossible for me to get my bearings from the sun, and I had no compass. I was helpless.

In riding down a slight incline while coming into the canyon, I had the misfortune of falling by riding into a rut. In doing so, I bent my handlebars so badly as to make them almost useless.

I could distinguish a little cabin a few miles up the canyon and started for it with the hopes of finding it inhabited, but upon reaching there, I found a deserted sheep camp. I was suffering terribly from thirst and had almost given up in despair when I discovered a little water hole a few yards from the cabin. Hunting around, I found an old tomato can, dipped some of the almost stagnant water, and drank it. This allayed my suffering to some extent, but my empty stomach still felt the want of nourishment very badly.

It was a barren and unsettled country that I was rid-

This little pumper, built in 1890, was the latest in modern transportation. Few Northwest farmers chose to ride the tracks on a Yellow Fellow wheel!

Photo courtesy: Union Pacific Railroad Museum Collection.

ing over at this time. The farmhouses were miles apart, and there were no towns on my route from Arlington to Echo, a distance of sixty miles. It is utterly impossible to raise crops through here, owing to the scarcity of rain and the strong west winds that blow continuously.

After drinking the water, I decided to retrace my steps down the canyon and endeavor to find the road that had led me into it, but I did not succeed. I then started in a direction that I thought would be east and made up my mind to go ahead until I came to a farmhouse. So, pushing my wheel up out of the gulch, I commenced to ride in every conceivable direction in a vain attempt at finding some kind of a road or trail. In doing so, I punctured my tires from the wireweed that grows so abundantly in this rolling country.

A few hours of this kind of maneuvering were sufficient to make me conclude to walk and lead my wheel. I had not walked far, however, before I found a road and, jumping on my wheel, rode on.

Everything went smoothly until I came to a small hill, which I attempted to ride down, but I was unable to control my wheel from sheer exhaustion. Consequently, I fell and broke the already crippled handlebars off at the neck. I did not know what to do or which way to turn. It was Sunday and the few farmers who manage to eke out an existence in this isolated country were at home. I picked up my wheel, placed it on my head, carried the handlebars (with the blankets strapped to them) in my hand, and started out to find a farmhouse.

I must have walked some four or five miles when I came to one situated at what is called Sandy Hollow and occupied by a family named Barthelamo. I asked for accommodations and was overjoyed at being answered in the affirmative. Mr. Barthelamo told me I was off my road and that I should have taken the old Oregon immigrant road at Wells Springs. This, of course, would have been an impossibility, as I had passed the Springs without knowing it.

Mrs. Barthelamo was an obliging lady and the possessor of a charming daughter, who had the effect of brightening my most lonesome and adventurous surroundings to some extent.

I learned there was a country blacksmith six miles east of Sandy Hollow on Butter Creek.

The following morning, September 2, found me up *Monday* long before the rest of the family. In the barn I constructed *Sept. 2* a wooden handle so that I could lead my wheel to Butter Creek. By this time breakfast was ready, and after partaking of one of those country meals consisting of salt pork, eggs, and pancakes, I bid the Barthelamos good-bye about seven o'clock and proceeded, leading the wheel with one hand and carrying the handlebars with the other.

Two hours passed before I reached Butter Creek. I had no trouble in finding the blacksmith, and after he had thoroughly examined the handlebars, he politely told me he did not see how he was going to fix them. I insisted upon his doing the best he could, and after much persuasion on my part, he concluded to do so. He managed to repair them so that I could ride very nicely. Truly, it was a clumsy piece of work, but appearances were out of the question at that time.

It was twelve o'clock when he had finished, and I decided to stay and have dinner before proceeding. Butter Creek is a small stream running north and south through a little valley not more than half a mile wide. It is like running out of a bed of thorns into a flower garden, to come down off the rolling country into it. While the country above is barren and desolate, this little valley is green with numerous orchards through it, and all because of this little running stream of water.

There are two kinds of inhabitants in Oregon, namely, the Web-Footers and the Sand-Winkers. I was among the Sand-Winkers at this time, and rightly they are named, for as I rode along after leaving Butter Creek I could hardly see the road on account of flying sand. A high west wind was blowing, which fortunately helped me along, but the roads were cut up pretty badly, and notwithstanding the favorable wind, I was unable to make very good time.

While the residents of rainy western Oregon have long been called "Web-Footers," the term "Sand-Winkers" for those in the arid eastern part of the state is one that my informants at the Oregon Historical Society have never heard. But, they allow, it fits.

There were a number of deserted farmhouses between Butter Creek and Echo. The land was taken up years ago by people of moderate means, and after trying year after year in vain to raise crops, they picked up their few belongings and deserted house and land. My curiosity was aroused by the genteel appearance of one of these houses, and upon entering, I saw a brand new stove standing in its place in the kitchen. Evidently the poor people were unable to carry it away when they departed for a more favorable location.

The wind still continued to blow, fiercer and fiercer, and I would have taken up my abode in one of those deserted houses had I had a supply of provisions on hand. But not wishing to repeat the previous day's experience, I concluded to go on. I reached Echo, fourteen miles from Butter Creek, at four o'clock, after having traveled at the rate of only five miles an hour, owing to the rugged roads, high winds, and flying sand. What an aggregation of difficulties, but this is what you may expect to experience when you wheel in eastern Oregon.

Echo is an almost deserted town, where they sell whiskey only by the gallon. It is not to be wondered at, as it stands to reason that a town cannot very well thrive when surrounded by deserted farms. My stay was of short duration, as I wanted to reach Athena, thirty-six miles from there, before night.

I was told to go directly east and did as I was directed, riding over hills and down through canyons. I found this sort of riding anything but pleasant, but I kept on until dark. Still being twelve miles from Athena, I concluded to turn into one of the many farmhouses along the road, as I had finally ridden into more prosperous farming country by now.

I chose one that I thought might be large enough to accommodate a stranger for the night. Mr. Struve, the head of the house, informed me that I would have to sleep in the barn, as his large family occupied every available room in the house. But after I told him where I was from and where I was going, he hustled around and made a bed for me in the garret. He was no exception to the rest of the Oregonians. He was the proud possessor of seven white-haired boys and girls, the oldest being only eight years old.

After partaking of my supper, consisting of hot bread

and milk with soup meat for dessert, I retired and found that my host had provided a very comfortable bed for me. I slept very little, however, owing to the youngest Struve keeping up a continuous howl all night, and was informed in the morning that the baby had never been so restless before. I concluded that I was the cause of the uproar and that the baby had never seen such a sight as I must have appeared that day.

4 *Some charming country . . . The luxury of a bath . . . That pesky prickly pear . . . Broken forks and a ball of twine . . . Singing in the rain on Mullan Pass . . . A bed unfit for a dog*

The following morning I was up and eating breakfast before daylight. As you are all aware, a farmer's work begins at sunrise and stops at sundown. This suited me very well, as I wanted to reach Walla Walla before noon. I was on my way at sunrise and reached Athena a little after seven that morning.

*Tuesday
Sept. 3*

Athena is a town of some fifteen hundred inhabitants and is situated in as fine a strip of farming country as one would wish to see. The soil is a rich black loam, and wheat is raised in great quantities—how very unlike the barren, deserted country I had just come over two days previously!

From Athena, I had great difficulty in finding the right road, owing to the many branches and forks that generally are the way in thickly settled farming districts. I managed to fall down a few more hills before reaching Milton, a small fruit shipping station on the Union Pacific, where I was told I was off my road three or four miles. I was directed to the right road and passed through some charming country, reaching Walla Walla at noon.

I went directly to the State [*Hotel*], where I enjoyed the luxury of a bath. The many downfalls I had been subjected to made me a fit candidate for one. As I was registering [*in those days it was customary for a guest to register even though he was only going to stop long enough for a meal or a bath before traveling on*], an army officer came running in to greet me, thinking I was the young private who had previously been sent on a bicycle with a message from Fort Walla Walla to Fort Vancouver and was expected home at the time of my arrival. In fact, I was mistaken for this soldier all along my route, as I somewhat resembled one with my canvas leggings and the Acme emblem on my cap, which farmers mistook for an eagle.

During my two hours' stay in Walla Walla, I was also interviewed by several reporters and was kept busy answering questions. You may rest assured I was very glad to leave at two o'clock in the direction of Spokane Falls.

I inquired the best way to go before taking my departure. A local wheelman informed me that the OR&N [*Oregon Railway and Navigation Company*] track was well ballasted with clay and was excellent wheeling.

I was about to leave by that route, when a farmer came along and told me I could save fifty miles by taking the wagon road, which according to his description was first class. Concluding that fifty miles was a large saving and worth taking advantage of, I started off on the wagon road.

It did not take me long to find out my mistake, however, as I found myself wallowing along in ten inches of dust in an attempt to ride over what Timothy Hayseed had called a first-class road. It was almost impassable, and to make matters worse, I had the opportunity of exercising my flying abilities while attempting to ride down some of the steep inclines. The thought of the bath I had taken haunted me as I went flying through the air and found myself lying full length in dust. A strong inclination toward blessing that farmer would take advantage of me.

This kind of road continued until I reached Prescott, a small town seventeen miles north of Walla Walla, at six o'clock and discovered that I had cracked the crown of my forks from the constant falling. I would have been handicapped, had it not been for the existence of a handyman in town who wired the forks and made them very nearly as strong as new. He charged me forty-five cents for his service, and I am wondering to this day why he didn't make it fifty.

Across most of Oregon Grandfather rode on the track, but here, southeast of Walla Walla, he went back to the wagon road—for obvious reasons.
Photo courtesy: Union Pacific Railroad Museum Collection.

The hotel accommodations at Prescott were very poor, and I retired that night a little fatigued after my first day's ride in the state of Washington.

I arose the following morning at five o'clock and was on my way twenty minutes later, concluding to get my breakfast at some section house up the road. The roadbed of the OR&N made excellent wheeling, but I had not forgotten the farmer who had so unmercifully started me off on the wagon road, when I should have been where I was that morning.

I was too early for breakfast at the first section house where I applied so, not caring to lose any time, I proceeded to the next one, designated on the map as Menoken. I found breakfast over, but the lady kindly cooked some eggs and warmed up some biscuits left over from the men's breakfast. She seemed very interested in me and the trip I had undertaken, as she was reading of McElrath and his wife on their bicycle trip around the world for the *Chicago Inter-Ocean.* She seemed to think he mentioned his wife too often, and it amused me when she was telling about it. I felt assured that she was not aware that poor McElrath had to write three columns a week for his paper, and in doing so found it essential to mention the New Woman as much as possible.

It was after eight o'clock when I bid the only woman of the section house good-bye and proceeded up the track. I had very good wheeling until coming to the Snake River, where I was compelled to drag my wheel over the rocks and railroad ties for a distance of five miles before reaching Riparia. There I crossed the river to Texas Ferry and went to the only hotel in town for dinner. Texas Ferry is another isolated spot, but there happened to be a pretty schoolteacher there that day, who had a tendency toward brightening the faces of the few old loungers that are generally seen around such places.

The railroad crosses the river at this point and runs up through the foothills of the Blue Mountains. Some of the old settlers tried to convince me that the wagon road was better wheeling than the track. Perhaps it was, but I did not care to find out the hard way again and decided to use my own judgment this time. I proceeded up the track, finding it tolerably good riding, and reached a farmhouse twenty-five miles north of Texas Ferry a little before sundown.

I applied for accommodations for the night, but I was told that the house was entirely too small for the large

You never knew what might roll into Winona on the OR&N tracks—a crazy fellow on a bicycle or maybe an agricultural demonstration train like this one.

Photo courtesy: Union Pacific Railroad Museum Collection.

family it had to shelter. I did not dispute their word when I saw half a dozen children clinging to their mother's skirts. Washington is very much like her sister state, Oregon, and claims to raise anything under the sun in large quantities. From appearances, she may rightly justify her claims.

I proceeded along the track and reached La Crosse Junction, a place consisting of a railroad station and section house a little before dark.

Thursday
Sept. 5

The following morning, September 5, found me up and away by six o'clock in the direction of Winona, ten miles distant. I was riding over a barren, unproductive strip of country now. Prickly pear, a species of the cactus, grows through here in large quantities, and it was over a bed of these pesky things that I ran soon after leaving La Crosse. This punctured both my tires.

I was compelled to lead my wheel until I came to a railroad watering tank, where I repaired them. Repairing tires had become a source of little consideration to me by this time, as I had experienced a great deal of inconvenience from punctures and was becoming accustomed to the art of repairing them.

The trademark of the Dunlop Tire Company, which had furnished the tires for the trip, was a pair of human hands —"These are the only tools you'll need." An ad in The Bearings *magazine December 5, 1895, expands on the theme: "We don't furnish a pair of pliers, a squirt gun, or a full supply of machinist's tools with each pair of Dunlop tires. Every rider is expected to supply his own tools, and unless Heaven has been unkind to him, he will find them growing on the ends of his arms."*

J. B. Dunlop, an Irish veterinary doctor, devised the first set of pneumatic tires for his son's tricycle, fabricating them from rubber sheeting and an old linen dress of his wife's. In 1889 he made an improved version for a friend who was a bicycle racer in Belfast. Both tires and friend were winners, and almost immediately the Dunlop Tyre Company was in business.

Apparently eager to break into the American market, Dunlop tried a variety of attention-getting schemes. In 1894 it modified a standard bicycle frame to seat the rider ten feet above the ground; this "Eiffel Tower Bicycle" cruised the streets of New York as a promotional stunt. Seeing a similar opportunity in Grandfather's ride, the firm was probably more interested in publicity for its tires than in his "accounting of their stability."

Riding along again, thinking my troubles were over for a time at least, I accidently ran into a hole and flew over the embankment against a large boulder. Upon recovering from the shock I had received, I examined 'my wheel and found that I had broken the forks where they had been wired up at Prescott.

I was now thirty miles from Colfax, the only place where I could have the forks repaired. Fortunately, I had a ball of large-sized twine in my bag, which I used to good advantage. The forks held, though very much under protest. The roads to Colfax were excellent, and it was fortunate for me that they were, as I could never have succeeded in riding over rough roads with my wheel in the condition it was. I arrived at half past twelve with my forks hanging by a thread.

I found a very good repairer there and had him mend

the forks and handlebars. As he consumed the rest of the afternoon doing so, I amused myself in the company of a number of local wheelmen. I met a young man who had his wheel rigged up to sit on the railroad track, and I had the singular experience of riding several miles on it.

Colfax is a very pretty little place, situated in a sort of hollow. On coming into town by the wagon road, you find yourself away up on one of the many high bluffs that surround the town. It is in the heart of the famous Palouse country, which is claimed to be the richest farming country in the world. The town has two thousand inhabitants, four banks, two daily newspapers, and many small manufactories.

The chief tourist attraction around Colfax at that time was an imposing hotel built by one James S.

Opening day at Cashup Davis's folly on remote Steptoe Butte. In spite of the hotel's grand ballroom and telescopes, those crowds never came again.

Photo courtesy: Julia Eckhart.

("Cashup") Davis on remote Steptoe Butte in 1888. It boasted a theater, a ballroom, and a cupola with a fine telescope, through which guests could see for 150 miles. Few guests came, but old Cashup lived there in splendor until he died, the year after Grandfather rode past. In 1911 the hotel burned to the ground.

The following morning I was on my way to Spokane Falls at seven o'clock and experienced the first frost of the season. I passed close to Mount Steptoe, on top of which is the Davis Observatory, and proceeded to the foothills of the Coeur d'Alene Mountains. Here I had difficult wheeling, but managed to reach Spokane Falls at five o'clock.

Friday Sept. 6

I had been on the road nearly a month by this time and had traveled over twelve hundred miles.

Colfax, Washington, "a very pretty little place in the heart of the famous Palouse country." Barely visible on the horizon is Steptoe Butte.
Photo: Bill Walter Photography.

Spokane Falls, 1895. Grandfather stayed only a few hours, long enough to "attend to various little nicknacks" and be entertained by the local Athletic Club.
Photo courtesy: Spokane Public Library.

Owing to the numerous delays from worn-out tires, broken forks, and so on, my stay in Spokane was limited to a half day. On arriving, I discovered that I had worn out one of the ball cups on the rear wheel. I endeavored to have a new one turned but did not succeed, owing to the machine shops' being overcrowded with work, which compelled me to proceed with a disable 1 wheel.

I was a guest of the Ware Brothers, well-known dealers in sporting goods, during my stay there, and in the evening I was entertained by the Spokane Athletic Club.

The next day's Spokane Chronicle *reported his arrival, adding the incidental information that "since starting on the road his appetite has become normal again, and he now eats his three square meals voraciously."*

*He seems not to have explained the (to him) hu-
miliating details of his friend Cornell's decision, for the*
Chronicle *stated, "When he started a companion accompanied him, but the latter got homesick when they
reached Sacramento and returned to San Francisco
again."*

*Grandfather should have taken in the local base-
ball game the day he was in Spokane. That same issue
of the* Chronicle *reported the score:*

	R.	H.	E.
Plainsifters	37	30	5
Portlands	24	23	9

The following forenoon was occupied in answering *Saturday*
letters and attending to various little nicknacks so essential *Sept. 7*
on a trip of this kind. Shortly after noon I was continuing
my eastward journey. The Ware Brothers advised me to go
to Missoula, Montana, by way of the old Mullan Pass and
the Missoula Cutoff, instead of going around by the main
line, and thereby save considerable distance.

My first stop was Coeur d'Alene City, Idaho, at
which place I arrived at three o'clock, after riding over
thirty miles of the finest roads. I passed within two miles
of the famous Indian battleground where General Wright
in 1864 ordered the slaughter of two thousand ponies, in
order to defeat the Indians. It is a well-known fact that an
Indian is helpless without his pony, and it is said that the
ground thereabout is covered to this day with the dry
bones of the unfortunate beasts.

Coeur d'Alene City is beautifully situated on the
Coeur d'Alene Lake and has a population of eight hundred.

Lake Coeur d'Alene as it looked that summer of 1895. Through a chain of connections—Spokane International to steamer to Northern Pacific—the mines were supplied.
Photo courtesy: Museum of North Idaho.

It is the chief shipping point to the famous Coeur d'Alene mines, connections being made with the S&I [*Spokane International Railway*] branch by steamer for the Mission, and there with the Coeur d'Alene branch of the Northern Pacific Railway, for the principal points in the mines.

Fort Sherman, which was established in 1879, is also situated there and contains five companies of the Fourth Infantry. I decided to stop at Coeur d'Alene City the rest of the day and, in doing so, visited the fort and learned some interesting facts about a U.S. soldier's life.

I registered at the Bancroft Hotel and found my host a very entertaining conversationalist. He was an old settler, and I was very much absorbed by his description of early life in Idaho. This was Saturday, and a number of the boys rode over from Spokane to spend Sunday on the lake.

The Coeur d'Alene Cycling Club was apparently less restrictive than the Acme boys. Curiously, Grandfather's journal makes no mention of this group at all.
Photo courtesy: Museum of North Idaho.

Their company combined with Mr. Bancroft's made it one of the most pleasant evenings I spent on the trip.

On arising the following morning, I discovered that *Sunday* it was raining. This was Sunday, September 8, and I felt *Sept. 8* somewhat blue as I thought of the preparations going on at Sacramento for the Admission Day celebration. [*September 9 is still observed as a state holiday in California.*] Nevertheless I concluded to proceed after being informed of the existence of large pine and cedar trees along the road I was to pass over, which would have a tendency toward sheltering me somewhat.

I had now commenced to go over that far-famed Mullan Pass through the marvelous Coeur d'Alene Mountains and found it anything but pleasant. The Mullan Pass government road was built by Lieutenant Mullan in 1864. An appropriation of $100,000 was made for the building of it; the lieutenant used $80,000 of it and returned the remaining $20,000. What an honest fellow he must have been!

Grandfather followed roughly the same route as today's Interstate 90. However, he crossed the Bitterroot Mountains through the old Mullan Pass, now called St. Regis. The pass that presently bears Mullan's name is farther north, but in 1895 there was no road across either it or Lookout Pass, where Interstate 90 runs. Today, on the other hand, no road remains over the old Mullan Pass where Grandfather rode.

The rain had not detained me much. Very true, it was somewhat annoying—but nevertheless I managed to keep on. Occasionally I would stop and sit under a tree and wonder what the boys were doing at home, until the rain would abate somewhat, when I would continue my lonesome journey. It was indeed a lonesome place with only pine and cedar trees for company.

Often I would lift the monotony of my dreary surroundings by singing some favorite song. To be sure, I took very good care that no one was in hearing distance, for there was the possibility that someone might take me for a blue jay or some other musical winged bird (so plentiful throughout these parts) and perhaps take a shot at me.

I reached the ranch of Mr. Clapp, twelve miles from Coeur d'Alene City, at half past ten o'clock, wet through to the skin, and asked permission to dry off. Upon receiving a favorable reply, I entered the log cabin and was soon sitting comfortably by the stove. By the time I had dried sufficiently, dinner was ready and the rain had abated.

After dinner I concluded to proceed. Mr. Clapp gave me some dry matches, so that if I got wet again, I could build a fire under a tree and dry off, as the farmhouses are few and far between in these mountains.

I had not gone far when it commenced to rain again, which compelled me to seek shelter under a tree. I was about to exercise my vocal accomplishments once more, when a two-horse wagon drove up. The wagon contained a well-to-do farmer of Washington who had been to Yellowstone Park and was returning home. He informed me that he had come through snow on the high elevations and did not think I could get through with my wheel. But as this was early in the season, I had no fear and, bidding my informer good-bye, proceeded on my way.

Good water flows in every conceivable direction in these mountains. As it rushed down the jagged rocks, it seemed to bring sweet music to my ears. I was walking along (it was impossible to ride owing to the rugged condition of the road) when I came up to three immigrant wagons standing on the roadside. Something had broken on one of the wagons, and they were repairing it. The occupants looked at me in amazement as I came up, for wheelmen are very scarce through this wild country, especially on stormy days. An old fellow, whom I picked out as the head of the combination, asked me where I was going. He laughed outright when I told him and asked me if I was going to ride that thing, pointing at my wheel. I replied in the affirmative and was about to continue when he yelled out, "Say! Tell them thar New York fellers to come out and see the big trees we have here. Tell them that you have to take three d——n big looks before you can see the top."

This little incident happened previous to my entering the famous Fourth of July Canyon, an indescribable stretch of road, through which I had difficult riding. Just picture a deep, rugged ravine walled in by high mountains with a small creek running through it. It is through this ravine that part of the Mullan Pass runs, and in many places the water runs over the road, forming ponds. I had to wade through these ponds as it was utterly impossible to pick my way along the side, owing to the thick growth of timber and brush so abundant in these mountains. Since the time of the railroads, the Mullan Pass has been neglected, a few straggling immigrants being the only ones to pass over it, until now it is almost impassable.

Carl G. Krueger, president of the Museum of North Idaho, provides this interesting bit of history: "The Fourth of July Canyon name can be traced back to the building of the same military road that runs over Mullan Pass. Apparently a construction crew, as part of their July 4 celebration, blazed a good-sized white pine tree about two feet from the ground and carved "MR (for Military Road) Jly 4 1861" on the blaze. This tree stood until the fall of 1962, when it broke off in a windstorm. At that time the carving was barely legible, but in 1895 it must have been very clear. Your grandfather would have gone by within a few feet of the tree."

I was wet from head to foot after getting through the Fourth of July Canyon, and to make matters worse, I was running into adobe [*Grandfather's California term for clay*].

This prevented me from riding, which I could have done had it been dry. I presume it is useless to tell you, dear reader, what adobe is after a rain. No doubt you have all experienced it sometime or other, either with team, on foot, or with a bicycle. It compelled me to stop quite often before reaching the Coeur d'Alene Mission.

This almost deserted town is at the head of the lake, and the commencement of the Missoula Cutoff of the Northern Pacific Railroad. The few inhabitants had heard of me through the Spokane papers and seemed deeply interested when I told them of my experiences in the Fourth of July Canyon.

I reached Kingston that night after a hard day's travel of thirty-five miles through canyons, high elevations, and last but not least, a drizzling rain.

There is only one place at Kingston where a traveler can be accommodated, and that is a farmhouse. Unfortunately, I found it one of the worst on the trip, and the inhabitants were extremely sarcastic. I was wet, cold, and hungry when I reached there, and upon entering the house, I found there was no fire in the sitting room. I asked them for a fire, at the same time telling them of my condition. They procured a log and threw it on the smouldering ashes, while I sat and watched it smoke. I was just commencing to lament on the unlucky state of affairs, when a woman's head popped round the door and called out in a snappish manner, "You can have supper now if you want it." I humbly answered that I was very much in need of the nourishment and so ate a meal consisting mostly of pork and beans.

After supper, I went over to the store to make a purchase and found the storekeeper very agreeable company. An excellent fire was burning in the large wood stove, so I concluded to stay there until bedtime in preference to spending the evening with the farmers.

The bed I slept on that night was unfit for a dog, let alone an unfortunate wheelman who was undergoing the hardships I was compelled to undergo at that time. When I retired, I found myself among a mass of broken springs and filthy blankets. I managed to forget all about it, however, and went to sleep praying for better weather the following day.

5 *Drunken miners and a mountain "rat" . . . The miseries of Montana mud . . .*
Bump, bump over the rocks . . . Monstrous and beautiful mountains . . . Where I
used bad judgment . . . A night with a toothless and talkative lady

Daylight dawned bright and clear on the morning of September 9, and after eating a breakfast consisting of pancakes and some beans left over from the previous meal, I proceeded on my way over surprisingly good roads, considering the heavy fall of rain the previous day. *Monday Sept. 9*

I traveled along the south fork of the Coeur d'Alene River and passed within a mile of Wadner, one of the principal mining towns in Idaho. As the buckets of ore would slide along the trolley on their downward course from the mountains to the smelters along the river, it made a very interesting scene.

The roads continued to be good all the way to Wallace, at which place I arrived at noon. It claims a population of twenty-five hundred, and the repair shops of the Northern Pacific Railroad are located there. The town is beautifully situated in a hollow, somewhat similar to Colfax, Washington. The mountains that surround it are covered with a growth of pine that remains green all the year round.

While I was eating dinner at a restaurant, a large crowd congregated around my wheel, and it was amusing to hear the ridiculous remarks they made. They were arguing as to how I rode down one hill and up another. Had they seen me flying down hills on the Oregon prairie, they might have drawn a correct conclusion.

One o'clock found me taking my departure from Wallace. Shortly after leaving the town of Mullan, I had to climb over the highest summit in the Bitterroot Mountains. I could only climb fifty feet at a time owing to the grade, which was at an angle of forty-five degrees. I had a mile of this kind of work. On reaching the top, I expected to see snow, but the little that had fallen the previous day had melted. As I descended over the rocks and boulders, I would talk to myself in order to alleviate the lonesomeness of my surroundings. I had difficult work in holding my wheel back owing to the steepness of the grade.

On reaching the bottom, I was informed that I had left Idaho after commencing my descent and was now in Montana. Here I had to ride between the rails once more, as the railroad company had laid its track over the grade that had cost the government $80,000. The poor immigrants have to haul their wagons over the railroad ties. Where there are trestles, they have thrown logs and stones in the openings to prevent their horses from falling through. This is the state of affairs along the St. Regis River in Montana.

I reached Saltese that evening at half past six, had supper at a section house, and found sleeping accommodations at a nearby log cabin that serves as a saloon and lodging house. A crowd of drunken miners had possession of this place the night I stopped there, and their arguments amused me immensely the forepart of the evening.

But on retiring, I was unable to go to sleep owing to the racket they kept up. They finally dispersed, and I was soon in the land of dreams, in the heart of the Bitterroot mountains.

Before retiring, I was given a description of the mountain rat. It is said that they grow to an immense size and will eat anything from a piece of cheese to a man's hat. I was awakened during the night by something crawling over me. Thoughts of the rats came to me like a flash, and with a bound I was out of bed. Upon lighting the lamp, a sight met my gaze that brought forth a smile, notwithstanding the scare I had just experienced. There, sitting on his haunches, was a large tomcat, looking as innocent as a kitten. After recovering from my unnecessary fright, I blew out the light and slept the rest of the night with the cat for a bedfellow.

Upon arising the next morning, I decided not to leave Saltese until nine o'clock, owing to the heavy frost that had fallen during the night, which made it a bitter cold morning. *Tuesday Sept. 10*

I kept along the track following the St. Regis River for some six miles, when I came to the wagon road. Once more I decided to risk it. I had not gone far, however, before I came to an exceedingly high mountain, called in Montana a camel's hump, and you may rest assured it made me hump before I was safely over it.

Sandy Cameron's Ferry was reached in time for dinner, after I had passed over another one of these humps. Sandy was busily engaged in ferrying over a train of immigrants at the time of my arrival, which compelled me to wait some time for my noonday meal. I was rewarded for my patience with a bountiful repast of bread and milk and some cold salmon trout.

After dinner I was ferried across and proceeded up along the Missoula River [*now Clark Fork*] over sandy roads, passing through the little town of Superior. I reached an old stage station called the Milk Ranch before night, after riding sixty-two miles that day. Unfortunately, the Milk Ranch's accommodations were not of the best. I had some biscuits for supper that night that would have made excellent cannonballs.

Wednesday
Sept. 11 The following morning, September 11, I was on my way to Missoula, fifty-four miles distant, before sunrise. I had not gone far after leaving the Milk Ranch, when my bicycle chain parted. I thought I was in for another walk, but upon examination I saw that one of the rivets had merely slipped out. I was not long in repairing it, after which I proceeded over mountains and down into wonderfully beautiful and natural ravines, admiring the scenery that abounded on all sides of me.

I found it rather difficult to ascend one hill, but upon reaching the top I was rewarded by gazing on a scene that will leave an everlasting impression in my memory. The road runs along the side of a high mountain at this point, and the Missoula River can be seen for miles winding in and out through the mountains, until it flows at the base of the mountain I have just mentioned. The railroad lies along the opposite bank, and a train of cars looked somewhat like a caterpillar from where I stood. The snow-capped mountains in the distance formed a striking background for the entire scene. It was romance in itself.

This kind of scenery varied somewhat until I reached a farmhouse occupied by a German named Henry Brown, where I stopped for dinner. Henry was a sociable fellow, and I could not help but like him. He informed me that the railroad company was claiming every other section of land and was being sustained by the government. This entailed a great hardship for some of the poor farmers, who had taken up land and improved it, only to lose it after years of toil.

The New York Times *warned its readers in 1880 (June 4 issue) against the lure of free land: "A farm may be had for nothing if any man has 'grit' enough to clear a wilderness and endure the deprivation of those little conveniences and refinements which temper life in settled communities. But families long accustomed to the amenities of New England and the Middle States should remember that the public lands do not embrace any ready made paradises; that their development involves time and toil, occasional contact with rude and desperate neighbors."*

Throughout the West farmers, frustrated by unpredictable weather and markets, seemed to find a convenient scapegoat in the railroads, which were often enough guilty of manipulating freight rates and the other excesses of which they were accused.

I ate the first prairie chicken I ever ate at Henry's, together with cucumbers and other vegetables (which are considered a luxury in Montana). I managed to gorge myself so that I was hardly able to mount my wheel when I was ready to take my departure.

There was still thirty-four miles to be covered before reaching Missoula. The first ten was somewhat rugged, but after reaching the Missoula Valley, I had excellent roads the rest of the way. It started to rain when I was within twenty-six miles of Missoula, but I kept on and arrived at five o'clock, drenched to the skin.

I registered at the Hotel Kennedy, and after disposing of my wet clothes for dry ones, I started out to find someone that would repair my broken ball cup. I succeeded in having the leading gunsmith of the town turn me a new one.

Missoula is the third largest city in Montana and has a population of forty-six hundred. It is the distributing point for a large part of the country around. It has two banks, seven hotels, two daily and two weekly papers, and its own waterworks and sewerage system.

There are two large fertile valleys lying to the south and west of Missoula. The foremost, the Bitterroot Valley, is very productive. Grain, vegetables, and berries grow in great quantities. The Missoula Valley (the one I passed through in the rain) is equally productive. Four miles south of Missoula lies Fort Missoula, a military post of three companies of colored infantry and a band. Unfortunately, I cannot praise the inhabitants of Missoula for their hospitality or sociability, as they are the most selfish and unfriendly lot of people I ever met.

Friday Sept. 13

The storm had increased in fury during my stay there, and I was compelled to make the town my abode for two days. It was Friday, September 13, when I bid goodbye to the few acquaintances I had made during my stay and rode up through the canyon in the direction of Helena. The storm was not over, but I concluded to take a chance and perhaps ride out of it. I had learned it was only a local one, and besides, I had hopes of meeting a more sociable community than Missoula.

I had not gone far when I was confronted by a tollgate. An enterprising individual had macadamized a strip of the road for a mile or so and erected a tollgate at either end. He charged me twenty-five cents for the privilege of riding over it. I remonstrated with him for charging me the same rate he would charge for a horse and buggy, and he politely told me that the bicycle was fast taking the place of the horse and buggy. I then came to the conclusion that I had run up against another man who did not approve of the bicycle on business principles.

The rain did not interfere with my progress very much. To be sure the roads were somewhat slippery, but nevertheless I managed to keep going right along and reached Bonita, a small section house twenty-six miles from Missoula, a little before dark. I was informed that comparatively little rain had fallen at Bonita up to the time of my arrival, but during the night it rained continuously, which made my start the following morning anything but pleasant.

I had not proceeded far before I reached another strip of adobe. Owing to the heavy rain the previous night, I was compelled to ride the the railroad ties until the sun had dried the roads sufficiently to allow me to ride over them. I reached a dismal-looking little town called New Chicago shortly after twelve o'clock. *Saturday Sept. 14*

Montana has some of the most unaccommodating hotel keepers of any state in the Union, and it was one of them that I unfortunately came across at New Chicago. He did not greet me, as is the custom of hotel keepers, but stood looking at me in dumb amazement while I pushed my wheel through the door and stepped up to register.

I broke the silence by asking him when dinner would be ready. "Oh, I guess in a minute," he replied in a careless manner. I sat down, picked up an old schoolbook (daily papers were not to be thought of here), and amused myself by looking over its well-worn pages for an hour or more before the dinner bell rang.

I had become ravenously hungry by this time, and the bell had hardly ceased its most welcome sound before I was comfortably seated at one of the tables. I had not been seated long, however, before a brazen-looking woman came up from the rear and called out the bill of fare in such a manner as to make it utterly impossible for me to understand. I asked her to repeat it, and with a frown that brought her face to the verge of distortion, she did as I asked. "Bring me whatever you have," I impatiently replied, for I was too hungry to stop and solve that bill of fare as she called it out. After she had served me, I discovered that the dinner consisted of roast beef and boiled chicken.

It was two o'clock when I bid New Chicago good-bye, and I sincerely hope I may never have the misfortune to have to stop for another meal there. I had left the Missoula River a few miles west of New Chicago and was following along the Hell Gate River. From New Chicago to Garrison the roads were exceptionally good, but after leaving Garrison, I was compelled to ride on the railroad track again, as the Blackfoot River, which I was now following, was not bridged.

The roads in Montana are poorly kept up, and there are very few bridges over any of the streams. The larger streams are crossed by means of ferries. As the smaller ones are shallow, the farmers find little trouble fording them with their teams. But when it comes to fording them with a bicycle, it means taking off your clothes and wading across. I was not in need of a cold bath at that time, so I managed to get along as I have already stated.

I reached Elliston that night a little before dark, after riding seventy-five miles under difficulties. I was within

twenty-three miles of Helena and started for there the following morning, September 15, by the way of Douglass Pass.

Helena lies on the eastern edge of the Rocky Mountains, and in order to reach there from Elliston, I was compelled to go over another summit somewhat similar to the one I had crossed a few days previously in the Bitterroot Range. I reached the top with comparative ease, but upon going down the east side, it was bump, bump, bump over rocks, boulders, and every conceivable obstruction.

To say that the scenery here is magnificent simply suggests my lack of language in which to present a view of it to the reader. It is bold, picturesque, beautiful, and grand; it is beyond the pen of man to describe. Those monstrous mountains of solid rock, heaped and piled one on the other, thousands of feet high, indicate the wonderful formations of nature. Looking from the high elevation on which I stood that beautiful Sunday morning, I could distinguish several small buttes. With their rugged covering they resembled the Seal Rocks at the Cliff House [*in San Francisco*] when they are occupied by the sea lions.

It was some time before I reached the level country, but after doing so, I was not long in reaching Helena, at which place I arrived in time for dinner. It was Sunday, and naturally the streets were lined with loungers. As I rolled into town, I was the center of attraction. It did not take long for a crowd to congregate around my wheel while I was eating lunch at the Montana Restaurant. Indeed, the police had to clear a passageway for pedestrians to pass. The lady cashier would not accept any remuneration for my meal, as she considered myself and wheel a good advertisement during the short time I was occupied in eating. "Keep it," she said, "and I wish you luck on your journey."

I had the pleasure of meeting Mr. C. P. Connolly, a prominent lawyer of Helena. He had visited Yellowstone Park during the summer and kindly gave me a route as far as Livingston. He also rode out of town with me and showed me the right road.

After reaching New York, Grandfather wrote Mr. Connolly a letter and several postcards. The reply he received must have meant a lot to him, for he saved it the rest of his life.

The first place I passed was East Helena, where large smelting works are located, after which I rode on to the Prickly Pear Valley, a very fertile stretch of land fifteen miles wide and twenty-five miles long. A strong southeast wind was blowing at the time, and together with the cobblestones that are strewn all over the road through the valley, it made exceedingly rough wheeling. I crossed the Missouri River for the first time, two miles west of Townsend, at which place I arrived a little before dark and registered at the Commercial Hotel. I retired at nine o'clock, feeling a little fatigued after a sixty-nine-mile ride over mountains and cobblestones and against headwinds.

Monday Sept. 16
The following morning I was away from Townsend at seven o'clock. The adobe roads were terribly cut up from the previous rain and had become dry. It was very much like riding over glass, and I discovered that it was cutting my tires up pretty badly. Twelve miles of this kind of riding brought me out of Prickly Pear Valley.

At Toston, another small town on the Missouri River, I crossed again and rode over twenty miles of prairie without a drink of water. I was so thirsty when I reached

Three Forks that my tongue was hanging out of my mouth.

Three Forks is an almost deserted town of fifty inhabitants. It derives its name from three rivers, namely, the Gallatin, the Jefferson, and the Madison, all of which empty into the Missouri at this point. I reached Logan, a small town six miles from Three Forks on the Northern Pacific Railroad, in time for dinner.

I was at the head of the pretty little Gallatin Valley, the richest and most fertile valley in Montana, at one o'clock and reached Bozeman at half-past four. Bozeman is the largest town in the Gallatin Valley and is situated on the East Gallatin River. It has a population of thirty-five hundred.

I concluded it was too early to stop for the day and inquired for the road to Chestnut, the next place on my route. I was told to keep to the main traveled road and was shown the canyon through which I was to pass.

I managed to get along pretty well until I reached Fort Ellis, an old deserted fort; here I turned to the left instead of taking the right-hand road. I kept on the wrong road for a mile or more before I discovered my mistake, being on a road which ran very nearly parallel with the one I should have taken. In order to save time, I concluded to cut across through the brush that divided the two roads instead of turning back.

Here is where I used bad judgment, as I could have ridden to Bozeman and returned during the time I was struggling through that one-fourth mile of brush. Everything went all right for a while, but after getting halfway across, I discovered a small creek, through which I was compelled to wade. I quite forgot to inquire into the depth of this creek. Consequently, I reached the other side looking more like a drowned rat than a transcontinental bicyclist. The brush was extremely thick on the other side of the creek and seemed to have a grudge against me. When I reached the opening, my shirt was torn completely off my back. I looked like a fellow shot out of a cannon, and all because of my persistence.

It was six o'clock when I regained the road, and I was only three miles from Bozeman, having consumed an hour and a half in making the distance. I was not long in reaching Rocky Canyon after I was once on the road and reached Chestnut at dark. There is some beautiful scenery through Rocky Canyon, and as tired as I was after the tussle with the brush, I was compelled to stop and admire it.

Chestnut is a comparatively new place, being only two years old. It is situated in the heart of Rocky Canyon and has extensive coal mines as its resource. The coal is not of the best quality, however, being soft and dirty.

I retired early that night as I was completely tired out from the seventy-five-mile ride, combined with the disastrous experience of going through the brush.

Tuesday
Sept. 17 The following morning I was up and on my way to Livingston at seven o'clock. I had very good riding until I reached Bozeman Hill, through which the Muir Tunnel runs. The tunnel was afire at the time I passed, and the railroad company was transferring passengers over the hill in the Yellowstone Park coaches, until they could build a track over the hill. It was a pleasant morning, and a number of the passengers were sitting on the side of the hill as I came along. After a sociable conversation with them, I proceeded over the hill and on to the adobe roads to Livingston.

I arrived there at half past nine o'clock and was informed that there were eight inches of snow in Yellowstone Park, which prevented me from carrying out my intention of visiting it. As usual, a large crowd soon gathered and asked me all sorts of questions. Among the crowd were a couple of newspapermen with whom I had a very pleasant chat.

I discovered that my tires were almost worn out, owing to the adobe roads I have already described. I had a new set in reserve at Miles City, but I did not care to wait for them to be sent back, so I took the chance of getting there with the old ones. Upon inquiring for the roads, I was told the best one was on the north side of the Yellowstone River, and after an hour's stay in Livingston I proceeded over excellent roads. I had come to the conclusion that the worst of my trip was over and that I would have smooth sailing. But I was sadly disappointed, as you will see later.

My tire had commenced to give me some trouble after leaving Livingston owing to the large quantity of prickly pear that abounds throughout Montana and over which I must have run unawares.

I intended to get dinner at Springdale, but because it is situated back in the hills on the opposite side of the river, I passed it before I discovered my mistake. I then concluded to keep on and apply for dinner at the first farmhouse I reached. On I rode over hills and down along the side of the river, until I came to a farmhouse occupied by a farmer named Chapman. Fortunately, they happened to be late with their dinner that day, and I was just in time to enjoy an excellent meal.

I met a young lady from Ohio who was visiting the Chapmans at the time of my appearance there. She gave me an invitation to call on her at her home in Columbus when I passed through, but unfortunately I passed through the northern part of Ohio and missed the visit. I endeavored to repair my tires after dinner with my new lady friend as overseer but did not succeed. It was an impossibility to accomplish the task owing to the gift of conversation that my lady friend possessed.

It was a little after three o'clock when I bid the Chapmans good-bye and proceeded on my way. My tires commenced to flatten soon after leaving, which necessitated my using the pump every four or five miles. I was in the midst of the much written-of prairie dogs now and enjoyed their cunning antics immensely. As I would come close to a settlement of them, they would give a squeal and, with their stubby little tails wagging, disappear into their holes. Some of them seemed to be exceedingly tame and would let me ride within a few feet of them.

The first town I reached after leaving Farmer Chapman's was Big Timber. The only thing that this prairie town can boast of is a goodly supply of cobblestones. I had exceedingly difficult wheeling, both before and after reaching there.

Upon looking over the railroad guide, I saw that the next town was Greycliff, at which place I intended to stop for the night. But upon reaching it, I was disappointed by finding only a section house and a small store. I applied for accommodations at the section house but was refused, owing to the scarcity of room. The storekeeper kindly directed me to a family named Whiting, who lived three miles farther east. In directing me, he said, "Go along down the track until you come to dog town." I interrupted him and innocently asked him if I could not find accommodations there. I thought he would split his sides laughing at me. When I asked the cause of his merriment, he informed me that the "dog town" was a settlement of prairie dogs.

I left my informer with a smile still on his face and proceeded according to his directions, feeling pretty cheap after showing off my ignorance. I had no trouble in finding Farmer Whiting's and rode up in front of the little log cabin (the houses all through this section of Montana are built of logs) shortly before sundown.

I was met by a woman, whom I judged to be forty-five years of age. She was thin and toothless, and good gracious, how she could talk! I asked her if I could stay there for the night and was answered in the affirmative. "Supper is ready now," she said, when I had barely put my wheel away.

I entered the cabin and saw that there was only one room, which contained a writing desk, a double bed, a stove, a table, and some chairs. I learned that the head of the house had gone to the mountains that morning to work in a sawmill of which he was part owner.

While gathering information for this book, I had the pleasure of talking with Vera C. Horton, daughter of "Jim and Lib" Whiting, who said that her parents often took in people in need of shelter. She does not remember her mother's ever mentioning Grandfather's stay, perhaps because the good woman met with a tragic accident when Mrs. Horton was only five, twelve years after Grandfather was there. Lib Whiting was with her husband at the sawmill seven miles up Bridger Creek when it happened. She had gone out to call the men to dinner when her full skirt got caught in the saw. It severed one arm and cut the other one badly. She died of blood poisoning three days later.

I ate my supper and, after finishing it, went outside and walked around the rear of the cabin to see if there was not another room attached to it. I failed to see any, however, and on coming in again, I sat down in one of the rickety chairs and looked fervently at the only bed in the room. I was commencing to wonder where I was going to sleep that night.

The old lady did not leave me in wonderland very long, however, for as soon as she had washed the dishes, she pulled one of the mattresses off the bed and, laying it on the floor, made me a bed a little distance from the other. She then placed nearly all the chairs there were in the room between them and, throwing some clothes over them, made somewhat of a partition. She then bid me go to bed when I was ready and sat down to read the paper with her back to the beds.

I was not quite ready to retire, so I sat down and read the paper also. We sat there reading until ten o'clock, when the lady commenced to yawn and remarked that she guessed she would retire. Out I went on the pretense of looking at the stars and waited until she had turned down the light. Then I returned and laid my tired bones down for the night.

I was completely fagged out and wanted to go to sleep, but she insisted upon telling me of the country's resources, of her husband's sawmill, and so on. I would answer yes or no, but could hardly keep my eyes open. Oh, how I wished that partition could have been soundproof! I fell asleep at last and must have slept some time when I awoke with a start and heard my lady friend still talking. I must have been answering yes or no in my sleep.

6 *Hard night in a boxcar . . . Dancing Crows and the Yellowstone County Fair . . .*
Letting sleeping ferrymen lie . . . The Badlands—Nature with her back up . . .
The pleasure of eating with cowboys . . . A hundred-mile day

The next morning Mrs. Whiting showed me her pet *Wednesday* *Sept. 18* pigs and lambs by way of an appetizer for breakfast. After repairing my tires, I bid her good-bye and went my way.

The roads were very good for some distance after leaving there, but upon reaching a section that had recently been taken up, I found myself in the midst of another difficulty. The settlers had fenced in their claims and in doing so blocked the only road there was, which compelled me to carry my wheel around the enclosures. Owing to the prickly pear with which I had had previous trouble, I soon tired of this enjoyment and decided to take to the railroad. Unfortunately, it was poorly ballasted, and I was compelled to walk.

This sort of traveling was kept up until I crossed the Yellowstone River, sixteen miles from where I had stopped the previous night. Here I found good roads, riding with a slight east wind until I reached Columbus, a small town at the head of the Yellowstone Valley. The road was as level as a floor for a mile after leaving Columbus, but then it commenced to lead me into the foothills again. I climbed to the top of one hill and from there saw a gradual decline, which I started to back-pedal down. I had not gone far when I came to a sharp turn, with a steep incline leading into another gradual grade, similar to the one I had just ridden down. In my attempt at making the turn, I ran into a mass of boulders on the side of the road and smashed my front rim to pieces.

There I was, thirty-six miles from Billings, the only place where I could hope to have the rim replaced. I was completely discouraged and sat down on one of the treacherous rocks that had left me disabled. I felt very much like crying.

After sitting there for some time, wondering how I was to get out of the predicament I was in, I came to the conclusion that I would never get out of it sitting on a rock. So I picked up the wheel and walked down to the railroad track. I walked three miles before coming to a station, which was occupied by a rich cattle raiser and designated on the map as Rapids. The leading cattle ranges of Montana are situated in this section of the state.

It was after twelve o'clock when I reached there, hungry, tired out, and discouraged. I asked for dinner and was accommodated. The house was in charge of a young fellow named Brooks; the rest of the men were out on the annual roundup. Young Brooks would accept no money for the meal I ate, and after thanking him, I departed, going in the direction of Billings with my broken bicycle on my shoulder.

I had not walked far before a farmer drove along on his way to attend the Yellowstone County Fair being held at Billings. I asked him if he would please haul my wheel there. He kindly consented and invited me to jump in myself. I declined his liberal offer and informed him that I had started out to either ride that wheel or walk across the continent. He did not parley with me very long but drove on, while I proceeded with "shanks old mare" and walked the first twenty miles at the rate of four miles an hour, as I wanted to reach Billings that night or early in the morning.

The four-mile-an-hour gait was too much for me. When I had walked to within eight miles of Billings, I was completely exhausted and took refuge in a boxcar partly filled with hay that happened to be standing on a sidetrack. It was nearly eleven o'clock when I crawled into the car. Had it been earlier in the evening, I would have applied to one of the many farmhouses, as I was in the thickly settled part of the Yellowstone Valley at this time.

(The Yellowstone Valley was, until recently, part of the Crow reservation, and it has only been thrown open to settlers for a short time. Nothing can be raised in it without irrigation, but fortunately the Yellowstone River flows through the valley and furnishes an abundance of water. I was told that four crops of alfalfa can be cut there in one season.)

The night I spent in that boxcar was an extremely cold one. I endeavored to crawl in between the bales to get warm, but I found it decidedly uncomfortable, and I soon crawled out again and lay on top. I was sore from head to foot from the long, fast walk, which had brought a different set of muscles into play, and this, combined with the thoughts of my broken wheel, made it a most dreary and miserable night. *Thursday Sept. 19*

The next morning I was up long before daylight and

was so sore that I could hardly walk the remaining eight miles to Billings. I managed, however, although every step was torture to me, and reached Billings at half past seven o'clock, only to meet the disappointment of not being able to have my rim replaced. I immediately telegraphed to Chicago for the new rim and also made up my mind to make Billings my abiding place for the next five days at least.

Fortunately, the Yellowstone Fair was being held at the time, and fifteen hundred Crow Indians were camped in the fairgrounds, which went towards making my stay somewhat interesting. I was too lame to think of attending the first day, but the second day of my stay saw me out at the grounds witnessing the weird war dances, which went to make up part of the attractions of the fair. The horse races did not amount to much; indeed, according to my estimation it would have been a very poor fair had it not been for the Indians.

The Crows are one of the most industrious and civilized of Indians in the United States. Some of them are quite wealthy and own some of the largest ranches and cattle ranges in Montana.

Old Chief Papaquis, the head of the tribe, is said to be worth over $300,000. To be sure, he is far above the average Indian in intellect and cunning, and he never misses an opportunity to add to his already large fortune. He has a right-hand bower in the person of a Negro called Smokey, who has mastered the Crow dialect to perfection. Smokey puts on a great many airs while riding through the street giving orders here and there, and when a Crow wants any information, he goes to Smokey to procure it.

Billings had the appearance of a toy shop the first few

Waiting five days in Billings for a new front rim was tedious at best. Luckily, the Yellowstone Fair was on, and fifteen hundred Crows were encamped there.
Photo courtesy: Denver Public Library.

days of my stay. The Indians with their gaudy colored blankets thrown around them and their hats bedecked with feathers, the squaws with their papooses strapped on their backs, and the ponies decorated with beads and elk tusks, all gave the town a holiday appearance.

We will now go over to where they are camped and take a look at their tepees. Here we see some hundred or more tepees with their two little openings, one that they crawl in through, and the other at the top where the smoke crawls out. It is amusing to see a crowd sitting around one of the fires, smoking and arguing about the superiority of their ponies over those of their neighbors'. The Indians are great lovers of horseflesh and will give anything they may possess for a horse or pony when they take a fancy to it.

The fair closed Friday night, after which the Indians packed up and departed. We now see them with their tepees strapped on their ponies' backs, with the six poles that go to make a tepee dangling along behind. As I have already stated, an Indian can very nearly carry a house and lot on his pony. The Crows are no exception.

Sunday we had snow, and the rest of my stay in Billings was consumed in playing whist at the hotel. The boys told me I had better put runners on my wheel if I intended to reach New York.

Monday
Sept. 23
Sunday night my rim arrived. Monday morning I had it put on and was away at one o'clock. This was September 23. I had been delayed five days through my carelessness.

After leaving Billings, I was compelled to take to the track again because the road on the north side of the river was little used, it was not fit to ride over. While at Billings, I had sent to Miles City for the new tires I had in reserve, as I learned that it would take good tires to resist the rocks with which the railroad was ballasted.

After crossing the Yellowstone River by the railroad bridge a mile east of Billings, I entered the Crow Reservation—as fine a strip of land as one would wish to see. When opened [*to homesteaders*], it will be the means of thousands of families' making a good living. It extends from Billings to Forsythe, a distance of a hundred miles. There are no roads through it, and had it not been for the railroad, I would certainly have had a hard time.

I reached Pompey's Pillar [*Grandfather spelled it Pillow*], a section house thirty miles east of Billings, a little before dark on the first night after my necessary delay. Pompey's Pillar derives its name from a large, monumental-looking stone that stands alone about one-half mile back of the house. Clark, of the Clark and Lewis Expedition, who explored the Northwest in early days, discovered it and inscribed his name thereon. In order to preserve the inscription, the railroad people have placed an iron plate over it. During the Indian troubles a company of soldiers camped around it, and they literally covered the pillar with inscriptions.

The accommodations were very good at the section house, and I managed to spend a most enjoyable evening with the section men. The following morning, September 24, I was bumping over railroad ties and trestles at seven o'clock on my way to Forsythe. *Tuesday Sept. 24*

At Pompey's Pillar I was told to cross the river at Custer and go over to Junction City, where I would find a good road. Upon reaching Custer, I commenced to exercise my lungs in a vain endeavor to awaken the ferryman, who had charge of the only means of transportation at that point. After shouting for some time, I concluded I could make better time by preserving my voice and returning to the track again.

I had only ridden a short distance, when I came to a log cabin occupied by several colored soldiers. It was used as a shipping station for Fort Custer, thirty miles south of there. I passed through the Bighorn Tunnel shortly after leaving the soldiers and crossed the Bighorn River a few miles farther east.

Shortly after crossing the river, I reached a section house called Bighorn and stopped for dinner. It was beginning to get rather lonesome for me now, as the section men were all Swedes and Norwegians, and entirely unacquainted with the English language. I had derived a great deal of pleasure on the fore part of my trip from stopping and talking with the section men as I went along, but I had to reach a town before meeting any congenial company now.

I still kept along the track after leaving Bighorn and was compelled to bump over ties until I reached Forsythe, a little after dark.

I stopped at the American Hotel and had excellent accommodations. The proprietor advised me to cross the river from there and go up the north side of the river to Miles City. Seven o'clock the following morning saw me hustling the ferryman out of bed in order to be ferried across. I was charged fifty cents for my trouble, and I made up my mind not to awaken any more ferrymen and have them take revenge by overcharging.

The roads were very good for an unsettled country and, with a strong west wind blowing that morning, I managed to get along rapidly. It was indeed a desolate country that I was in that day, with a goodly supply of sagebrush and prickly pear as the only vegetation. A mass of barren, low hills added to its already weird aspect and made it surprisingly interesting to me.

Within twelve miles of Miles City, I stopped for a drink of water at what I thought to be a farmhouse. But after knocking at the door, I was confronted by a pretty little "school marm," who unhesitatingly supplied my wants, and I managed besides to have an exceedingly interesting conversation with her.

After bidding the schoolteacher good-bye, I was not long in reaching the river once more, where I had to be ferried across again. I was only charged twenty-five cents this time, owing to the fact that the ferryman happened to be awake.

I arrived in Miles City in time for dinner, passing Fort Keogh on the way. The town lies on the east bank of the Tongue River and is devoid of either ferry or wagon bridge. Thus I was compelled to trundle my wheel over the railroad bridge in order to get there. I had an excellent dinner at the Hotel Marquin, after which I resumed my eastward journey.

The wind changed around to the southeast in the afternoon. This fact, combined with the misfortune of losing my way a number of times before reaching Dixon, the first section house east of Miles City, made it a most difficult and disagreeable experience.

After leaving Dixon, I was compelled to wade through a number of irrigating streams, then entered a group of low-looking hills that shelter the numerous little valleys throughout this part of Montana. After I had made my way well into them, I discovered that I would have to walk, owing to the coarse gravel with which the roads are covered and through which it was utterly impossible to wheel.

In fact, I was coming to the extreme edge of the Badlands, and as I would ascend a hill and gaze around me, a weird-looking sight would meet my eyes. The stubby hills with their perpendicular sides appeared as though a huge meteor had grazed along them on its mad flight to Mother Earth. It was interesting to look at for a moment, but beauty was lacking, and I wished I were out of them. On going a little farther, I came to a large opening, and gazing down into the abyss below, the sight that met my eyes almost made my blood run cold, to think of the terrible force Nature has when she gets her back up.

I soon tired of this and returned to the railroad track, as it was getting dark and I did not care to get lost in the hills. After regaining the track, I proceeded and reached a section house called Shirleys, long after dark. The lady kindly cooked supper for me, and after eating a hearty meal, I retired completely worn out from the continuous struggle with hills and railroad ties.

I cannot say that I was enjoying the trip at this time, for I was not. Indeed I only wished I had never seen a bicycle.

Thursday Sept. 26 The blues had disappeared by the following morning, however, and after repairing my tires (this being my usual morning routine), I bid the few occupants of Shirleys good-bye and was on the road for another day of difficulties and adventure. I had ridden some thirteen miles when I concluded to learn the time of day, but upon feeling for my watch, I discovered that I had left it under the pillow at Shirleys. The roads were too rugged to think of returning for it, and as the section boss appeared to be an honest-looking fellow, I concluded to keep on and send for it from the next town. Fortunately, I met a pump repairer who gave me the assurance of its being all right. I failed to receive it, however, until I reached the end of my journey at New York.

After considerable bumping over railroad ties and an occasional ride over a side path, I reached Terry, a little town east of Shirleys, where I was informed that I could get an excellent dinner at Fallons, twelve miles farther east. I proceeded over pretty good roads to within half a mile of there when I met a cattle outfit and stopped for dinner.

Fallons is one of the principal cattle-shipping points in the Northwest, and at the time of my passing through, three thousand head were rounded up in the vicinity waiting to be shipped. It was at one of these roundup outfits that I stopped for dinner.

The cowboys eagerly asked me to share the noonday meal with them, and I was not sorry that I had accepted their invitation, as I had never had the pleasure of eating with cowboys before. Have you ever come in contact, dear reader, with a number of cowboys? If you ever do, you will never regret it, as they are the most whole-souled human beings on the face of the earth. To be sure, they are always playing practical, and sometimes serious, jokes on one another, but when one is in need, the others are always ready to lend a helping hand.

A roundup outfit consists of an ordinary farm wagon on which is set a large box fitted with a number of drawers, in which the necessary eatables and cooking utensils are placed while the cowboys are on the move. When stationary, they hang a large pot on three poles that are tied together at the top, and in this way they cook their soup, or whatever their meal may consist of, in a most inviting and wholesome manner. They use no tables and take what they have on tin plates, sitting Turkish fashion, and eat to their hearts' content. They eat in a much happier

Among the slides for our old family stereoscope I found this one of cowboys—a reminder perhaps of that happy lunch with the Montana roundup outfit?

mood than some that have all the luxuries of a modern dining room in a fashionable hotel.

There happened to be a son of an English nobleman in the crowd. His father had sent him out to this wild country to break him of his waywardness. The rest of the boys guyed him unmercifully on account of the strong English accent of his speech. I was told he was a splendid rider, however, but did not know enough to eat at the proper time.

Fallons has only a section house and a telegraph office. After passing them, I turned to the left and rode down to the river, to be ferried across for the third time. I then had thirty miles of good wheeling, combined with a favorable wind, to within one-half mile of Glendive. Here I had some trouble getting through the sand to the river. After reaching the water's edge, I had to yell for some time before I succeeded in gaining the ferryman's service to take me across the Yellowstone for the fourth and last time.

Glendive is a town of fifteen hundred inhabitants. The railroad machine shops are located there, and the inhabitants are exceedingly proud of the miserable bit of farming land that is in close proximity around it.

The Badlands proper begin at Glendive and end at Dickinson, North Dakota, a distance of one hundred miles. I met a number of drummers at the hotel, whom I had seen at different points along the road. They seemed surprised that I was getting along so fast through that rough country.

Friday Sept. 27 On the morning of September 27, I started on my hundred-mile ride through the famous Badlands.

Now I came to a succession of hills, somewhat similar to the ones I have previously described only much more pronounced. The Badlands were originally one vast prairie, the eruptions underneath having caused parts to fall away showing the different formations of the earth. At the top of one of the many hills or bluffs, a black loam can be seen. A little below that comes a gray clay, then a vein of earth resembling cinders. Under this we have a brick-colored earth, which goes to prove that intense heat is or has been in existence underneath. Taking it as a whole, it gives us a first-class illustration of what Nature can do when aroused.

In between the hills, some very good grazing land is found, and it is said that the cattle find first-class shelter along the sides of the bluffs during the severe winters that go to complete Montana's resources.

The first part of my ride was along the railroad, owing to the sandy condition of the wagon road, but after I reached Beaver Hill, twenty-eight miles from Glendive, I had excellent roads clear through. At noon, I reached Wibaux, another cattle-shipping point, and ate dinner.

I was about to resume my journey when I discovered that my handlebars were on the verge of breaking where they had been brazed at Colfax, Washington. I went to a blacksmith's shop, procured an L-shaped piece of iron, and wired it onto the broken side of the bars. Thus I managed to repair them temporarily and resumed my journey.

A strong west wind was blowing at the time, and after mounting, I had only to steady my machine and the wind did the rest. Very true, the roads were not of the best. They were rutty, and my wheel was under a heavy strain from coming in contact with the side of the ruts. Occasionally, I would find myself lying all over the road, but that did not matter—I was used to it now. Anyway, I found better roads in the Badlands than I had expected.

Sentinel Butte was the next stopping place after leaving Wibaux, and my ride between the two places was comparatively easy. Sentinel Butte is a section house and derives its name from a large hill that towers way above the rest and stands directly at the back of the house. It can be seen for miles around.

From Sentinel Butte to Andrews, another section house at a distance of sixteen miles, the roads are not so good, as the country is exceedingly hilly. The wind was blowing a gale, and I could hardly stand on my feet. From the top of the many high points I reached, I could look down into the depth below and gaze upon a sight that was bewildering as well as wonderful. I wondered what I was going to see next.

I reached Andrews a little before sundown. The accommodations were excellent, and the people endeavored to make my one night's stay as agreeable as possible. Indeed they seemed to be quite in love with my company. The lady had to make a bed for me on the floor, as travelers did not often stop there overnight.

The wind blew a perfect hurricane that night and will leave an everlasting impression on my memory of my one night's stay in the heart of the Badlands.

Saturday Sept. 28

The folks there expected snow, and that set me thinking as to whether I would have to prolong my stay or not. Fortunately, the next morning dawned bright and clear, and I was on my way to Dickinson before seven o'clock.

The next place after leaving Andrews is called Medora. It is situated on the Little Missouri River. Medora is the place where the Marquis de Mores, a French nobleman, undertook to show western cattlemen a thing or two by sinking two million dollars in a vain attempt at carrying on an extensive packing establishment in the heart of the Badlands.

I had a pleasant chat with the telegraph operator, who told me that Medora had been a lively place until the Marquis finally got onto himself and quit.

The operator seemed tired of his surroundings. I could hardly blame him, as Medora is one of the most dismal-looking places on the face of the globe. He asked me for information in regard to California fruit farms, as he intended to go there and invest in the near future. I gave him all the information I was capable of and resumed my journey toward the rising sun, following along the track to within four miles of Sully Springs, where I came to the road again.

I rode out of the worst of the Badlands and onto a hilly prairie at Sully Springs, continuing over the same kind of ground to Belfield, where I had dinner at the section house.

I had been sleeping and eating at section houses for two days now and had become somewhat used to them. The Belfield house was occupied by an Irish family. The nationalities differ through the Badlands. This Irishman was possessed of some half-dozen children, and on my entering the house, they amused themselves by throwing my wheel down and putting the finishing touches on my already crippled handlebars. This necessitated my hunting up another piece of iron and some more wire in order to get them in condition to go the remaining twenty miles to Dickinson. I finally managed to get them wired up so they would hold and reached Dickinson at three o'clock, with five spokes out of the rear wheel and a broken handlebar.

7 *The thriving saloons of dry Dakota . . . Patching up my forks once more . . .*
The miserable lot of the prairie farmer . . . An outrageous two dollars a night . . .
Broken spokes, strange roads, and one very angry Swede

The local telegraph operator found bicycle repairing quite profitable during his leisure hours, and it was to him that I was compelled to apply in order to have my rear wheel steadied up a bit. The rest of the afternoon was passed by the operator and me in accomplishing the most difficult undertaking of sticking tandem spokes into ordinary nipples, his supply of spokes being somewhat limited. Repairing the handles was out of the question—that was entirely out of his line of work. I was thus compelled *Sunday* to leave the following morning (Sunday, September 29) *Sept. 29* with the handles no better than I had fixed them at Belfield.

While at Dickinson, I stopped at the Villard House, a so-called first-class hotel, but I found it nothing more than an ill-reputed gambling den, where one could be accommodated with any game of chance.

North Dakota is supposed to be a prohibition state, but one can have all he desires in the way of intoxicating liquor. It is served from bars in the same manner as elsewhere. The state derives no revenue whatever, and it appears very much as if the saloon keepers were at the bottom of the prohibition.

The country in the vicinity of Dickinson is of a decidedly rolling nature, but not so much so that it prevented my making pretty good time. The road was first-class as far as Glen Ullen, a small town fifty miles east of Dickinson, at which I arrived in time for dinner. A Catholic church located here is the means of bringing farmers for miles around on Sunday to attend service. Some of them require two wagons to carry their families, owing to the yearly increase.

I rode pretty close to the railroad between Dickinson and Glen Ullen, but after leaving Glen Ullen, I left the track and entered into the hills. Now I saw an almost unproductive country; when I say almost, I mean that they raise a crop about once in seven years.

This part of North Dakota is mostly settled by Germans, whom the railroad company enticed out there by sending agents to Europe to offer every inducement to get them settled on its lands. After that, the Germans are left to eke out a miserable existence the best way they can. It is almost impossible for them to make both ends meet, owing to the severe winters that prevail in this part of North Dakota. They live in dirty, low adobe [*sod*] houses, which reminded me very much of the old missions in Southern California. I lost my way several times that afternoon and had great difficulty in finding it, on account of the settlers' inability to speak English.

Not only the railroads but the state, individual
towns, and private land companies all promoted the

glories of North Dakota to German immigrants. In fact, the capital was named Bismarck in the hope of attracting German investments.

I reached New Salem that evening at five o'clock. It was long before sundown, and I could have kept on, but as there is no town within twenty-eight miles of there, I concluded to stop for the night. I did not wish to be caught on the North Dakota prairie among foreigners after dark.

I was rewarded for stopping by meeting a young fellow from California. We spent a most pleasant evening talking over the advantages of the Golden State, and we both wondered that people live in such a barren state as North Dakota.

The next morning saw me on my way to Mandan, twenty-eight miles distant, before seven o'clock. By this time, my wheel was commencing to show the excessive riding it was subjected to; consequently, I reached Mandan with the front part broken in two. Unfortunately, Mandan was not possessed of a repair shop, which necessitated my going to a tinner, who plastered a piece of sheet brass over the break. When finished the front of my wheel looked as if someone had shot a ball of hot lead at it. It was the best I could do, however, and after eating a somewhat hurried meal, I proceeded in the direction of Bismarck.

After trundling my wheel over railroad ties for some three miles, I reached the railroad bridge—the only means of crossing the Missouri River at that point—only to be informed that I would not be allowed to cross. I was compelled to return to Mandan and procure a permit from the division superintendent, after which I crossed without further interruption.

It was three o'clock when I left Mandan the last time, and on arriving at Bismarck I discovered it was five o'clock. The distance between the two places is only five miles, and I could not imagine how I had come to consume so much time, but owing to the excitement of having my wheel repaired and the inconvenience of crossing the river, I had forgotten that the time changed—I had lost an hour between the two places.

Bismarck is the capital of North Dakota, and the capitol building is not much larger than a wealthy man's residence. There is an amount of rivalry between Mandan and Bismarck, as one can easily see when there is not even a wagon bridge across the river. The two cities each have a population of two thousand.

My stay in Bismarck was of short duration, as I failed to see anything there that attracted my attention. So I proceeded eastward, passing the state penitentiary—another insignificant-looking building—a mile from town. I reached Mendotan, the first section house east of Bismarck, after passing through some very good farming land, and stopped there for the night.

It was the first day of October when I bid Mendotan good-bye. Proceeding over excellent roads through Sterling, Steele, Crystal Springs, and Dawson, I reached Tappen, a station on the railroad put there for the accommodation of a large cheese ranch. None of the places that I passed through had a population to exceed two hundred. *Tuesday Oct. 1*

The folks I had dinner with at Tappen were exceedingly unsociable. I asked question after question as to the country's resources, and so on, but I was answered invariably in a snappish manner. I cannot account to this day for the unsociability of the North Dakotans. Perhaps they were

averse to bicyclists, or upon second thought, their surroundings might have had something to do with their lack
of hospitality. Indeed, I cannot blame them—just think of
sowing crop after crop, only to have them killed by
drought or burned up by prairie fires.

A great many of the towns I have mentioned are
boomtowns and are scarcely inhabited now. Poor people
went there and spent what little they had in a vain attempt
to raise a crop. Now they are compelled to stay and do the
best they can, while others more fortunate have picked up
and moved to more congenial localities.

The roads were miserable after leaving Tappen, being
somewhat sandy and rutty. After I had ridden some ten
miles or more I discovered that my forks were breaking
again.

Jamestown, fifty miles from there, was the only place
I stood any chance of having them repaired. I happened to
have a few spools of copper wire in my bag, which I put
into very good use, and succeeded in temporarily mending
them.

I managed to reach Windsor, another boomtown, seventeen miles west of Jamestown, a little before sundown
and stopped for the night. An English syndicate attempted
to make a city of Windsor and built a large hotel by way
of an enticer, "a la Southern California style." Their attempt was fruitless, however, and the hotel, with accommodations for three hundred guests, is now occupied by a
man and his wife who have a so-called farm in the vicinity.
A store and the station go to make up the rest of the once-
boomed city. I had the pleasure that night of occupying
one of the rooms in the Englishman's wild investment.

*The hotel no doubt did look large, sitting as it did
on the prairie with nothing around it but one- and
two-room buildings; but W. M. Leingang, photo cura-
tor of the State Historical Society of North Dakota, ad-
vises me that it actually had only thirty-five or forty
rooms —still pretty imposing for a community like
Windsor, North Dakota.*

The following morning I was up and away before five
o'clock, as I wanted to reach Jamestown and have my
wheel repaired so I could leave there at noon. It was a bitter morning, and I suffered intensely from the cold. This,
combined with the darkness that made it a near impossibility to find my way, made my situation exceedingly dis-
tressing.

*Wednesday
Oct. 2*

I reached Jamestown a little before seven o'clock and
had to wait some time for the repairer's shop to open, after
which I was informed of his inability to repair the wheel
owing to the absence of a brazing machine. He advised me
to send for new forks, but I hated the idea of waiting in
that lonely, forsaken country for the parts so told him to
go ahead and do the best he could.

After pondering over it for some time, he concluded
to make an attempt and succeeded somewhat in accomplishing a most unsightly piece of repairing. I also had
him give the wired-up handlebars a good application of
solder by way of a preventive. After having eight spokes
put in the rear wheel, I was ready to continue my journey
once more.

True, my wheel was a sight, but appearances counted
for little with me at that time, and I was beginning to

have grave fears that the wheel would not carry me through. At any rate, I intended to ride until it would carry me no longer, when I would have given it up for a bad job and have charged it to the wheel.

After partaking of a hurried dinner, I bid Jamestown good-bye at half past two o'clock and proceeded against a strong southeast wind. The wind had the effect of retarding my progress to some extent, but notwithstanding I managed to reach Sanborn, a little prairie town twenty-six miles east of Jamestown, a little before sundown. Unfortunately, I stopped at one of the worst hotels I had stopped at on the trip. I could scarcely get enough to eat, and that, combined with a carpetless floor, a hard bed, and not enough blankets to keep me warm, left a very unpleasant remembrance of Sanborn in my mind. The proprietor had the audacity to charge me at the rate of two dollars a day for the accommodations.

Nowhere have I been able to learn how much money Grandfather was carrying or what measures he had taken to keep it safe. The only reference to the matter, and hardly a credible one, was in the Stockton Daily Independent, *which said:*

"Each man carries a pair of blankets, a camp cooking outfit, a gun and $5 in money. They did not take a greater supply of the needful, because they intend making expenses along the road. They will do advertising for various firms and, as they are both bright and have had some experience in the journalistic field, will write letters for several papers."

They did indeed carry blankets and gun, and both men were bright enough (Cornell's decision to turn back is enough to qualify him as far as I'm con-

*cerned). But there is no evidence that Grandfather
ever intended to cook out or earn money along the
way, or that he ever sent any letters back to newspapers. And even at 1895 prices, that five dollars would
surely have been gone long before he reached the
Oregon border. It's just possible that he concocted the
whole story to avoid being robbed.*

I was up the following morning at five o'clock and intended to ride to the next place for breakfast. But owing to
the light supper the previous night, I came to the conclusion that I was too hungry to proceed and waited until six
o'clock for breakfast. This meal was far worse than the
previous one; indeed, I had to run the feet very nearly off
the poor, unfortunate waiters before I could get half
enough to eat. It was nearly seven o'clock when I had paid
my bill and was ready to continue my journey against
another southeast wind. I also managed to lose my way,
which compelled me to cut across fields and climb fences
before reaching Valley City, a town somewhat larger than
Sanborn.

On arriving at Valley City, I stopped for a drink, and
in doing so I was accosted by some North Dakota farmers.
They asked me what I was riding for. When I told them I
was out for health, pleasure, and adventure, they did not
seem to see any sense in riding across the country on a
wheel for any such purpose and declared they would rather
walk. I came to that conclusion also, as I could not see
how they could invest in a wheel when they only raised a
crop once in seven years, and nine times out of ten the
chances would be of that being swept off by a prairie fire
before it could be harvested.

Valley City is nearly as large as Jamestown. It is pret-

*Thursday
Oct. 3*

tily situated in a canyon and cannot be seen until you reach the brow of the hill before descending into the town. It has a population of fifteen hundred, and the town is supplied with water from the Sheyenne River, which flows through it. The state normal school and a branch of Keeley's Institute for the cure of drunkenness are located there.

After a hot argument with some Keeley graduates on the liquor question, I left Valley City and proceeded up the Canyon for one-half mile, after which I turned left and rode under the Soo Line [*Minneapolis, St. Paul & Sault Ste. Marie Railway*] trestle. I managed to lose my way again and did not know it until I had come to an obstruction—a house occupied by an old Irish woman. She directed me to the right road, but I succeeded in getting lost again before noon.

The country is somewhat level after leaving Valley City, and one can see the settlements or towns along the railroad for miles. But the wagon road diverges from the track at intervals and connects with forks or branch roads that run in every conceivable direction. This was the means of bewildering me to a great extent, hence the pleasure of losing my way a number of times before reaching Buffalo, a town of five hundred inhabitants, in time for dinner.

I had dinner at one of the so-called poolrooms and restaurants combined. They are nothing less than the lowest of rum shops, with the sign "Poolroom and Restaurant" over the door for a blind, in order to evade the law. I can say without exaggeration, that North Dakota contains more saloons in proportion to its population than any state in the Union, and still it is called a prohibition state.

As he crossed North Dakota, Grandfather seemed to be equally critical of the illegal saloons and the temperance fanatics. Probably he was disturbed more by hypocrisy than alcohol, because he was not a teetotaler himself, although in the journal he admits to drinking whiskey only for medical purposes. My uncle Frank recalls that he kept a bottle of Old Crow on hand (the only liquor in the house) to be trotted out when business associates would call. He always drank it straight and never had more than one drink.

The wind had gained in velocity while I was eating dinner, and as I emerged from the saloon, preparatory to taking my thirty-six-mile ride to Fargo, it was blowing almost a gale.

The country is as level as a floor between Buffalo and Fargo, and the roads are excellent. Wheat is raised in large quantities, and the farmers could be seen for miles around plowing for the spring sowing. I was commencing to ride through the farming portion of the state at this time, which had the effect of making my surroundings somewhat pleasanter. It is impossible to raise a tree on those prairies owing to the severe winters, and one does not have the pleasure of gazing on any foliage until Fargo is reached. Even there trees are what might be called a scarcity. How different from beautiful California, where the farmer is not compelled to plow in the fall in order to get his crop sown as soon as the snow is gone in the spring, and where the beautiful foliage can be seen on all sides, growing to dizzy heights and proportions! How I longed to get only one glimpse of California's trees as I rode over these treeless prairies!

I reached Fargo that evening a little before six o'clock, after passing through Casselton and the famous Dairymaple ranch. This ranch consists of twenty-five thousand acres under cultivation. The soil is a rich, black loam, and wheat and flax are raised in large quantities.

The roads were excellent, both after leaving Casselton and while passing through the ranch, but I was completely exhausted from the continuous strain I was subjected to while proceeding against the wind.

The North Dakota race was being held at Fargo on my arrival, and the city was crowded with visitors. I had a little difficulty in finding accommodations but succeeded at the New Fargo Hotel. I had ridden seventy-five miles that day, and I was commencing to go through better country and over better roads. This gave me some encouragement, notwithstanding the battered condition of my wheel.

Fargo is the metropolis of North Dakota and claims a population of ten thousand. It is situated on the famous Red River of the North, which divides North Dakota from Minnesota. The authorities are very strict with the prohibition law in Fargo and will allow no saloons to run openly, as is the case in the smaller places through which I passed. One can get all he wants, however, if he knows the ropes; and if he is a stranger, all he has to do is to walk over the Red River bridge to Moorhead, Minnesota, where he can quench his thirst in a jiffy.

I had followed the Northern Pacific Railroad from Spokane Falls to Fargo, a distance of 1,261 miles. I was advised to leave it at Fargo and follow the Great Northern, as by so doing I would avoid the sand through which the Northern Pacific runs east of Fargo.

I left Fargo and North Dakota on the morning of October 4. It was but a few moments after leaving that I crossed over the Red River bridge and into Minnesota.

After passing through Moorhead, I turned to my right and rode over exceedingly level country in a southeasterly direction. Sabin was the first town I reached on the Great Northern. I only stopped there for a drink of water and, proceeding on, reached Barnesville, where I commenced to ride over rolling country once more.

At Barnesville I inquired for the road and was advised to follow the track, when I should have kept away from it for some three miles. I did not discover the mistake until I had run into a swamp where there were no roads whatever. I endeavored to ride after reaching the swamp, and in doing so ran into a large hole, breaking five more spokes out of the rear wheel. This was a sufficient cause for making me walk the remaining three miles to Lawndale, the next station, where I was directed to the right road.

Lawndale consists of a grain elevator and a store. I was informed that the occupants of the store fed travelers, should they happen along at mealtimes, and as it was noon, I applied for dinner. The cook happened to be indisposed that day and politely offered me some cheese and crackers. I did not propose to wrestle with a bicycle over bad roads on a diet of cheese and crackers, so I proceeded to Rothsay, twelve miles distant, and had an excellent dinner at the Rothsay Hotel.

When I inquired for the best road to Fergus Falls, the next important town, the hotel proprietor willingly informed me that I would have to go six miles south then turn and go seven miles south again. I looked at him in amazement but did not dare to say anything for fear that I might be laughed at for my ignorance, not knowing but what that was the Minnesota style of directing a stranger over strange roads. I mounted my wheel and proceeded in a southerly direction with the intention of solving the road question myself.

I was in the farming country now in every sense of the word, with vegetation on all sides of me. Consequently, there were numerous roads running in every conceivable direction. This part of the state is settled mostly by Swedes and Norwegians, which made it difficult to find my way, owing to their inability to speak the English language. This was indeed a most serious predicament, as I discovered after leaving Rothsay.

After I had pondered my situation for some time, a German farmer, who had mastered the English language to some extent, came along and advised me to keep straight ahead until I saw the smoke from the asylum at Fergus Falls. I took his advice and proceeded for some distance but saw no sign of smoke.

I was beginning to lament my ill luck for not being supplied with a field glass, when I discovered a dark line of smoke rising heavenward to my left. How to get over there without taking the wrong road was another question for me to solve. The first turn I made brought me up to a farmhouse, where I found that the road ended. This necessitated my return to the main road for another attempt.

I had the unsought-for pleasure of repeating this a number of times before reaching Fergus Falls, at which place I arrived at five o'clock, after having to wade through a number of creeks on the way. Just as I was riding into town, a Swede commenced to swear at me in his native tongue for scaring his team. I failed to understand what he said, and perhaps if I had, there would have been a row, as I was not in the best of humor at the time.

8 A ride through Norway and a few unavoidable falls . . . The bicycle brass band . . . Minneapolis and St. Paul . . . The Mississippi . . . High bluffs and steamers plying . . . Frost on my whiskers and twenty miles of sand

Fergus Falls is a pretty little place of five thousand inhabitants, beautifully surrounded by lakes and timber. The great Red River of the North flows through it and furnishes valuable water power, running a number of manufactories. One of the state's insane asylums is located there and can be seen for miles from the surrounding country. It is said that 99 percent of its inmates are Swedes and Norwegians. I failed to go through it, however, owing to the condition my wheel was in and the lateness of the season, which necessitated my not losing any more time than I could possibly help.

It was long before sundown when I arrived there, so I decided to ride to the next town, twelve miles distant and designated on the map as Dalton.

It is useless for anyone to go to Europe on a wheeling tour when he has the same opportunity to wheel through it in America. I had gone through a little Germany in North Dakota, and now I was traveling through Norway and Sweden. I would ask ten- and twelve-year-old, white-headed, American-born children questions in regard to the roads and distances from town to town, only to be stared at in a frightened manner, as they could not speak a word of English. What an unacceptable state of affairs in our glorious republic. Our free schools have thrown open wide their doors for the education of our children, only to see them grow up unable to speak or understand the English language. This is what I saw in the farming districts of Minnesota, and I could hardly believe it.

The state of Minnesota can boast of more beautiful lakes than any state in the Union. They are mirrors of magnificence surrounded by forests of maple, oak, and cedar. At the time I passed through, the trees looked their prettiest, with variegated leaves that reminded me of that beautiful song, "When the Leaves Begin to Fall." I was continually riding out of one pretty scene into another.

I had traveled some ten or twelve miles after leaving Fergus Falls, and it was becoming quite dark. The moon was just rising and cast a weird shadow over the magnificent scenery I was passing through. As I rode along thinking of the many amusing incidents that had happened during the day, I saw ahead of me what I thought was a farmer driving the cows home to milk. Imagine my surprise upon riding up to him to find him taking advantage of the bright moonlight and plowing with the cows. Anxious as I was to reach Dalton, I dismounted and watched him. It was useless to attempt to converse with him, however, for I was traveling through America's Norway.

After a short stop, I moved on through the forest and along the beautiful lakes with an occasional necessary dismount, owing to some lazy polecat crossing the road. I was not in a position to bury what clothes I had on my back.

After a few unavoidable falls down steep grades (owing to the darkness and my ignorance of the roads), I reached Dalton at half past eight o'clock and registered at the Great Northern Hotel. Supper was over, but the proprietor kindly got me a cold lunch, after which I retired, somewhat fatigued from my first day's ride in Minnesota.

Saturday
Oct. 5

The following morning saw me taking my departure in the direction of Ashby. The country is exceedingly hilly after leaving Dalton, which made it difficult wheeling, but the beautiful scenery more than repaid me for the inconvenience, so I called it even.

After reaching Garfield in time for dinner, my next stop was Alexandria, where I endeavored to have the five spokes that I had broken the previous day put in. I did not succeed, however, and proceeded to Sauk Center.

Small towns all across America seem to have posed for their portraits on the Fourth of July. This is Osakis, Minnesota, in the lake country.

Photo courtesy: Minnesota Historical Society.

From Alexandria to Osakis the road is as fine as one could wish for with numerous summer resorts all along, which made my ride over this strip of road a very pleasant one.

After leaving Osakis, I rode along Osakis Lake over a boulevard. After that the roads are only what might be called passable to Sauk Center.

I reached the latter place at five o'clock and succeeded in having the spokes put in. My old clothes and shoes were looking pretty shabby by this time, as I had worn them clear from California. Since I was fast coming into civilization, I concluded to improve my appearance by purchasing an entire new outfit. I continued my journey the following *Sunday* morning, Sunday, October 6, in the direction of St. *Oct. 6* Cloud.

From Sauk Center to Melrose I had excellent roads, but after leaving there I had to walk through three miles of sand to Fremont. From Fremont to Albany I had sand at intervals. From Albany I rode on to higher ground and had better roads to Avon. From Avon to St. Joseph the ten miles of road was almost impassable.

The timber was exceptionally thick all along my route through here and resembled the Rocky Mountains scenery to a nicety.

I learned upon reaching St. Joseph that a party of wheelmen had ridden from St. Paul to St. Cloud the previous evening and that they intended to return that afternoon. I hurried on in order to have company to St. Paul. It was an exceedingly fine road, and I reached St. Cloud at two o'clock—only to be informed that the wheelmen had departed on their homeward journey two hours previously.

St. Cloud is a city of over twenty-eight thousand inhabitants. It boasts a bicycle brass band of twenty-four pieces, and from the pictures that I saw of the band while on parade, it was indeed amusing to see the many difficult positions they must acquire in order to play and at the same time propel their machines.

More than anything else in the journal, except perhaps for the Acme boys themselves, I have wanted to find a picture of this bicycle brass band. Unfortunately, all my efforts, even to inserting an advertisement in the personals column of the St. Cloud Daily Times, *have yielded nothing. We can only imagine how grand they were!*

After a hearty dinner at the Grand Central Hotel, I crossed the Mississippi River and rode down its east bank along the railroad track. I reached Elk River, a small lumbering town, at dark and registered at the Riverside Hotel.

The next morning, October 7, saw me leaving Elk *Monday* River for my thirty-six-mile ride down to St. Paul. I *Oct. 7* should have crossed the Mississippi River here and gone down on the west side instead of riding down the east side as I did. By so doing I would have avoided the sand, through which I had hard work making headway. I managed to reach Anoka, but was directed onto seventeen miles of worse road before reaching Minneapolis.

It is useless to attempt to describe Minneapolis. All I can say of it is that its businessmen are most enterprising, wide-awake, ever ready to grasp every opportunity that comes their way and at the same time make the best use of it. There is a great deal of rivalry between Minneapolis and St. Paul, but nevertheless Minneapolis is far ahead in every respect. One can ride the ten miles between the two cities on the interurban electric road for the small sum of ten cents.

My stay in Minneapolis was of short duration, there being no agent for my wheel there. As the wheel was sorely in need of an overhauling, I was compelled to ride over to St. Paul. I spent the two days I had to wait (while my wheel was being repaired) with friends in Minneapolis.

Wednesday Oct. 9 At noon, October 9, my bicycle was in readiness, with a new front wheel, new handle, and new forks. I left St. Paul by the way of West Seventh Street and crossed the high bridge over the Mississippi River. I then turned south in the direction of Cannon Falls, but owing to an exceedingly strong south wind that was blowing that afternoon, I was compelled to change my route and go in a southeasterly direction toward Hastings, losing my way a number of times. There I stopped for the night, having only ridden twenty-six miles that afternoon on account of the wind.

This was an entirely different route from the one I had decided on at St. Paul, as I intended to go to Cannon Falls, then to Zumbrota, and from Zumbrota directly east to La Crosse. Instead I rode down along the bank of the Mississippi River. To be sure, the roads were not as good as the ones I had previously decided on, owing to the sand that is invariably found along the banks of the river, but the beautiful scenery I saw along the Mississippi more than repaid me for my exertions.

Thursday Oct. 10 The following morning I had not gone far before I ran into a bed of sand, which was the means of compelling me to walk some four or five miles. After reaching the ridge, I proceeded over better roads, reaching Red Wing at ten o'clock and Lake City, forty miles from Hastings, in time for dinner.

III

Lake City lies on Lake Pepin, a very pretty body of water, thirty miles long and three miles wide. The road runs along the side of it for some distance before reaching the town, and the scenery along its shores are beyond description. The high bluffs, the pretty little valleys, and the steamers plying from shore to shore make a scene that leaves an everlasting impression on one's memory.

After seeing Lake Pepin, I left Lake City and had to climb a two-mile grade in order to reach the ridge road again. On reaching the top, I saw some of the prettiest farms in the country, and as I rode over the rolling land, a feeling of contentment came over me which enabled me to enjoy the ever-changing panorama that was continually meeting my gaze.

The steamboat "Quincy" landing at Redwing, Minnesota, ca. 1898. Grandfather felt that the scenery along the Mississippi "more than repaid me for my exertions."
Photo courtesy: Minnesota Historical Society.

I proceeded, with the river in sight, to Kellogg, where I was advised to take the ridge road, as I would have considerable sand to contend with along the river. I did contrary to the advice, however, owing to the many difficulties I had previously had in finding my way through the farming districts. I continued along down the river, finding the sand as it had been described to me, which necessitated my riding along the railroad in a great many places.

Friday
Oct. 11 I managed to reach Minneiska that night a little before dark, registering at the only hotel in town. I arose early the following morning and made my way over miserable roads to Minnesota City, where I had breakfast. The towns were very close together now, and I often arose early and proceeded to the next one for breakfast in order to improve my appetite.

From Minnesota City to Winona, the roads were the best, and I reached the latter place at nine o'clock. It is an exceedingly pretty place of twelve thousand inhabitants and is one of the many thriving little towns on the Mississippi River.

At La Crosse, one of the largest cities in Wisconsin, I crossed the river and bid good-bye to Minnesota and the beautiful Mississippi. After partaking of dinner at the Mitchell Hotel, I called on some of the local wheelmen in order to get a route to Milwaukee. I had been told of the Wisconsin sand while passing through Montana and was trying to avoid it. They could give me very little information, however (as was the case with all wheelmen with whom I came in contact, owing to the fact that they had never ridden more than twenty miles out of town).

I then concluded to go to Milwaukee via Viroqua,

Sauk City, and Madison, and after bidding the wheelmen good-bye, I departed from La Crosse at half past twelve o'clock.

The first thirteen miles of my ride was over excellent roads. Then I had to climb another grade for a mile and a half to the ridge road, after which I had rolling country to Viroqua, thirty miles from La Crosse, where I stopped for the night. It is useless to describe the scenery I passed through that afternoon. Space will not allow it; it was magnificent beyond description.

Wisconsin is mostly settled up with Germans, and a thriving people they are, who raise enormous crops of tobacco every year. My abiding place at Viroqua was at the Park Hotel. I met a party of tobacco buyers there, and a jolly good crowd they were. We spent a most enjoyable evening singing and playing. They seemed deeply interested in my trip, which compelled me to answer a good many questions before retiring.

The following morning I was up and on my way *Saturday* before breakfast, long before the tobacco buyers thought of *Oct. 12* arising. I went in the direction of Viola, fourteen miles distant, at which place I arrived hungry enough to eat the town out of all the available eatables. It was a bitter cold morning, and the ice had formed on my whiskers. It was anything but comfortable, but I enjoyed it to some extent as this was my first experience with real cold weather.

Though many people in the nineties resented the bicycle, it had its enthusiasts, too. Among the many virtues they claimed for cycling was its benefit to health. And judging from an article that appeared in the New York Times *on November 25, 1895— while Grandfather was in New York—the colder the*

*weather, the healthier the sport. Headlined "Cold
Weather Suggestions and Tips for Cyclists," it said:
". . . Admitting that it does require some forti-
tude to brunt the northerly blow, the fact remains to be
urged that it pays to do so. For the majority of persons
much real benefit is to be had from riding under these
very conditions, and there is, too, more genuine sport
and satisfaction in it. In the first place, the defiance
and conquest of the elements are something. It is a
great deal for nerve-worn and moody men. Such mas-
tery creates exuberance; it gluts the pride and self-
reliance. Next, deeper breathing is indeed induced, and
the air consumed in less time than in the milder season,
while the general toning and invigorating efficacy of
the exercise are greater.*

*"Another decided advantage in braving the blast
is that it cultivates nasal breathing. Americans have
been dubbed a Nation of mouth breathers. This is unkind discrimination from the British Isles, but the fault
is prevalent here, and it is never more effectually
checked than when rushing through cold air on a wheel,
practically doubling the wind's velocity by riding
against it. As no one can endure drawing the icy atmo-
sphere direct into the lungs, the art of keeping the
mouth closed and breathing solely through the nostrils is
learned. This habit, once formed, quickly becomes
fixed, so, if it be chosen to carry the point to flippancy,
rough weather might be recommended as a cure for
snoring—another National accomplishment.*

*"Nor do the arguments outlined apply only to
hardy individuals, but as well to the less robust riders,
including women. Better than nostrums and cosmetics*

is it for the gentle sex. It gives clarity and color to the skin and lustre to the eyes, and if a bit of chappiness is involved, it is more than compensated for by the buoyancy of step on the ballroom floor that will come from the work. . . ."

The article was just in time, for a weather forecast elsewhere on the page indicated that the city could expect snow. Other items of interest reported the organization of a new cycling club, the Queens County Wheelmen; an announcement by the New York Central that bicycle fares, already being protested as too high by riders, would be raised to 20 percent of first-class fare; and the defeat of American cyclist "Zimmy" Zimmerman by an Australian named Parsons in a "five-mile scratch," after which "the crowd was so excited that it rushed on the ground and carried Parsons off in triumph."

From Viola, I rode over good roads to Richland Center. There I endeavored to get a route to Sauk City from some of the local wheelmen, but they were unable to give me directions or any information in regard to the roads. This necessitated my applying to some of the farmers, who advised me to go via Spring Green, a little town on the Chicago, Milwaukee, and St. Paul Railroad. Here is where I made a mistake, as a farmer has not the least idea of a road when it comes to cycling. I should have kept along the ridge road, whereas the farmers sent me down through twenty miles of sand. After struggling through it and reaching Spring Green, I discovered that I was way south of Sauk City and on a direct line with Madison. This necessitated my changing my plans once more. I decided to go to Madison by way of Arena and Mazomanie.

I followed along the Chicago, Milwaukee, and St. Paul, still through sand, until I reached Arena, where I stopped for the night. *Arena* is an Indian word that translated means "sand." You may rest assured that the word fitted the place to perfection.

9 *Chicago . . . Marble-Heart Barrett of "The Bearings" . . . Cider and singing with the Hoosiers . . . A companion lost to the wind . . Apples, oil wells, and bitter cold A teetotaling wheelman in search of a temperance hotel*

The following morning dawned bright and clear, and after partaking of a hearty breakfast, I left Arena, still going through sand until I reached Mazomanie. From there I had the best of roads clear to Madison, where I arrived at noon.

Sunday Oct. 13

It was a beautiful Sunday morning when I rode into Wisconsin's capital city. I was not sorry that I had undergone the many hardships I had in order to reach there on a bicycle. Indeed, I was enjoying the trip immensely now, as I was over the worst of it. The rest as you will see, was constant pleasure in every sense of the word.

I met a number of wheelmen at Madison, among them Mr. C. Tyner, who rode to Sun Prairie with me, where we had an excellent dinner at Mr. Connor's Hotel.

From Sun Prairie, I followed the Chicago and Northwestern Railroad as nearly as possible. The difficulties in finding roads were over, as lines of telegraph poles connect all large cities on the main roads. I reached Ocon-

A bicycle livery in Sheboygan, Wisconsin, ca. 1900. In his 4,354 miles Grandfather visited several such establishments—and numerous blacksmiths in between.
Photo courtesy: State Historical Society of Wisconsin.

omowoc that night and registered at the Jones Hotel, one of the handsomest hotels in the Northwest. Oconomowoc is a summer resort for Milwaukee's and Chicago's Four Hundred. It is beautifully situated on a number of small lakes—so abundant in Wisconsin—and affords good boating in summer and excellent duck shooting in winter. Rockefeller, the Standard Oil king, is counted among Oconomowoc's summer residents.

Monday Oct. 14   The following morning I left Oconomowoc for my thirty-six-mile ride to Milwaukee. I had breakfast at Hartman, after a spin of ten miles by way of an appetizer. The towns are quite numerous along here, being only three miles apart, which made my ride between Oconomowoc and Milwaukee a most pleasant one. I still used the telegraph poles for a guide passing through Waukesha (from which the famous Waukesha water was piped to the World's Fair) and reaching Milwaukee at eleven o'clock.

After three hours' stay in Milwaukee, consumed in visiting friends who had been former residents of the Pacific Coast, I proceeded south along the lake [*Lake Michigan*] to Racine. I arrived at dark and registered at the Hotel Mohr. Racine can boast of more manufactories for the size of its population than any city in the United States. It has the best shipping facilities either by rail or

Oconomowoc, Wisconsin, summer playground of millionaires. For one glorious evening at the Jones Hotel, Becker's Market seemed far, far away.

Photo courtesy: State Historical Society of Wisconsin.

boat and has a population of ten thousand.

The following morning I bid Racine good-bye for my sixty-five-mile ride to Chicago. Keeping along the west road to Kenosha, I proceeded thence along the lake road, passing through Waukegan and Fort Sherman, and had dinner at Highland Park. After dinner I rode over Sherman Boulevard to within sixteen miles of Chicago. Here we have Evanston, and then the beautiful Chicago boulevards, which lead into Lincoln Park. The famous ferris wheel is on my right (not mentioning the one in my head). I reached the Wellington Hotel, where I registered, at four o'clock. My ride from Madison to Chicago had indeed been a pleasant one, and I was really glad that I was living.

I stayed a day in Chicago, owing to some repairing that had to be done on my wheel. The bearings had commenced to wear, and spoke after spoke would break out of that troublesome rear wheel. I had the pleasure of being introduced to "Marble-Heart" George Barrett of *The Bearings* and several other newspapermen during my stay in Chicago. The season was getting extremely short, which necessitated my leaving much sooner than I would have done under other circumstances—I had a delightful time while there.

I had the good fortune of meeting company at the hotel in the person of Mr. C. P. Parkhurst, a prominent wallpaper dealer of Toledo, Ohio, who asked permission to accompany me on my eastern journey as far as his home. I was overjoyed at the thought of having such congenial company as Mr. Parkhurst appeared to be and gladly accepted.

We bid Chicago good-bye on the morning of October 17 and rode out on Michigan Avenue to Sixty-third Street,

As he rode in on "the beautiful Chicago boulevards which lead into Lincoln Park," Grandfather noted the ferris wheel on his right. Noteworthy indeed!

Photo courtesy: Chicago Historical Society.

following that street to Stoney Island Avenue. Here we could see the ruins of the once-beautiful White City, where I had spent six of the happiest weeks of my life only two short years before. After viewing the wreck that fire and dynamite had administered to the mammoth World's Fair buildings, we followed along Stoney Island Avenue until we reached Pullman. A short stop was made here in order to view the extensive car shops of the Palace Car king.

From there we were advised to ride in between the double tracks of the excellently ballasted Michigan Central Railroad. It was indeed a godsend that we were so advised, as we had intended to take the wagon road. This would have compelled us to drag our wheels through forty-two miles of sand, for which eastern Illinois and northern Indiana are noted. As it was, we had excellent wheeling between the tracks, passing through Hammond and Kent, Indiana, on the way. It was exactly two o'clock when we arrived at Chesterton and decided that we had better have something to eat after our forty-two-mile ride.

We had passed the sandy country by this time and decided to take the wagon road. From Chesterton we rode through a beautiful farming country, with an abundance of corn stacked up on all sides. This had the effect of making my ride a most enjoyable one, and together with Mr. Parkhurst's company, you may rest assured that I was a study of contentment.

Indiana is noted for the hospitality of its people, and we did not miss taking advantage of it when we were invited into some of the cider mills along the road in order to test the superiority of one factory's cider over that of another. As Mr. Parkhurst would smack his lips after gurgling a glass of new cider, he would invariably say, "God bless the Hoosier State!" We soon tired of testing cider, however, and reached La Porte at five o'clock.

Registering at the Teegarden Hotel, we spent a most enjoyable evening in company with a number of drummers, singing and telling funny stories until after midnight. On arising the following morning, we felt somewhat tired for the want of sleep, but notwithstanding we were away at seven o'clock. We rode over excellent roads and reached South Bend at ten o'clock; here we stopped for refreshments, then proceeded to Elkhart for dinner. *Friday Oct. 18*

A strong southeast wind had blown up by this time, and my companion was commencing to complain. He was not as young and supple as myself and found it exceedingly

The Teegarden House, La Porte, Indiana. In 1940, after eighty-eight years of hospitality, it was torn down; a Woolworth store now occupies the corner.

Photo courtesy: La Porte County Museum.

The Teegarden dining room must have seemed positively elegant after Oregon section houses, Dakota saloons, and potluck in many a farmer's kitchen.
Photo courtesy: La Porte County Museum.

hard work riding against the wind. After a short rest at Elkhart, we resumed our journey, but we had not gone a mile from town when my Toledo friend informed me that he would have to return and take the train, as it was an impossibility for him to propel his machine against the wind. Indeed, I felt sorry to think that he had failed to keep up, and I continued on alone bewailing my ill luck in not being able to keep a companion. Very true, the wind was blowing a gale right in my face, but I had experienced the same up north, and I did not intend to weaken at this stage of the game.

The roads were very good, which was one point in my favor, and I managed to reach Brimfield a little before dark and registered at the Hotel Crum. Mr. Crum, an old Grand Army veteran, entertained me immensely with his interesting war stories and, together with his charming daughter, made it one of the most enjoyable evenings of my journey.

The following morning, October 19, I was away immediately after breakfast, but not before I had bid Mr. Crum and his daughter good-bye. How I would have enjoyed that trip, had I met more such people as I met at Brimfield! They were full of kindness and wished me Godspeed on the rest of my journey as I left on that Saturday morning with a favorable west wind and signs of a storm approaching. The roads were all that could be wished for, and I reached Bryan, Ohio, in time for dinner. *Saturday* *Oct. 19*

At Bryan, I discovered two kinds of time, sun time and standard time. Both existed through the northern part of Ohio and were the means of getting me muddled up more than once. When I reached Bryan, it was twenty-five minutes to twelve by the town clock (my watch was back in Montana). But, the workingmen were all going to dinner, which made me question a bystander as to the clock's correctness. He explained the situation, saying that the working class commenced and quit work by sun time, which was twenty-five minutes slower than standard time.

My next stop after leaving Bryan was Wauseon. Here I inquired for the road to Perrysburg, at which place I was to strike the famous Perrysburg Pike. I was directed to Napoleon over twelve miles of the finest pike road I ever rode on. Ohio is noted for her piked roads, as I was told of them away up in the Northwest. Now they were indeed a reality.

After reaching Napoleon, I was directed down the south side of the Maumee River. I was very much surprised in not finding sand along its banks as I had along the banks of all the rivers I had followed. Apples grow abundantly along this river. All I had to do was to pick them off the overhanging branches as I went along and eat to my heart's content. Such delicious apples they were that I almost made myself sick by partaking too freely of them.

That night I reached Grand Rapids, twenty-five miles southwest of Perrysburg, and registered at the only hotel in town. The accommodations were excellent, however, notwithstanding the absence of competition. I was told I could cut off some distance by leaving Perrysburg to the north and cutting across the country to Woodville.

I acted accordingly and left Grand Rapids and the Maumee River the following morning, Sunday, October 20. The roads were excellent to Tontogany, seven miles east, and together with a slight, exhilarating breeze that was blowing from the south, enabled me to ride along without fatigue.

From Tontogany to Woodville the roads were miserable, being very little used. It is between these two places that Ohio's oil wells, with their weird-looking towers, are located. These were not so beautiful to gaze upon as the scenery I had previously passed through, and I was very much relieved when I reached Woodville and left them behind me. I came to the Perrysburg Pike at Woodville and followed it to Clyde, where I had an excellent dinner at the Empire Hotel.

The roads now were all that could be desired. At Oberlin, I found a bicycle path eighteen miles long to Elyria, reaching there a little before dark and obtaining excellent accommodations at the American Hotel.

It had turned pretty cold as I rode into the pretty little village of Elyria, and I expected to see snow upon arising the next morning. I was disappointed, however, by only seeing a heavy frost. It was half past six o'clock when I had eaten my breakfast and was ready to take my departure for a twenty-six-mile ride to Cleveland.

I suffered somewhat from the cold, but nevertheless I managed to reach there at nine o'clock and discovered that I was minus eight spokes in that troublesome rear wheel. I proceeded straight to the Ohio Supply Company for repairs, and they succeeded in getting the wheel in shape at the appointed time—twelve o'clock. I continued on my journey following Euclid Avenue until I reached the outskirts of the city,' where I had dinner at one of the suburban restaurants adjoining the Lakeview Cemetery. *Monday Oct. 21*

After dinner I entered the beautiful cemetery and visited the Garfield Memorial, one of the handsomest structures of its kind in the United States. It is built entirely of granite and stands one hundred and eighty feet high. It is surmounted with a handsome dome fifty feet in diameter at its base. The price of admission is placed at ten cents, which goes to defray the expense of keeping it in repair. One can get a good view of Cleveland from the top of the dome, which is reached by a spiral staircase. Garfield's body lies in a beautiful copper casket that stands in a room on the extreme lower floor. His mother's remains lie in an adjoining room but cannot be seen. Taking the surroundings as a whole, it leaves a lasting impression on one to view the last resting place of the immortal James A. Garfield.

After visiting the monument, I proceeded over miserable roads. At Willoughby, I inquired for the best roads in the direction of Buffalo. Mr. Yaxley, the popular hardware man of Willoughby, kindly mapped out a route for me as far as Geneva.

As I have already stated, I expected to see it storm at Elyria, some forty miles west, and had been disappointed. My disappointment was relieved somewhat, the farther east I went, by riding where it had snowed the previous day. The roads were almost impassable from the melting snow. It retarded my progress to some extent, but I managed to wade through the mud and water until I reached Madison.

Tuesday
Oct. 22 I was wet from head to foot as I entered the Park Hotel at Madison and registered for the night. A huge fire was burning in the old-fashioned fireplace in the hotel office, and I was not long in monopolizing it. I concluded to stop there until the roads had dried up some.

A strong north wind arose during the night, which had the effect of drying the roads considerably, and I was enabled to continue my journey the following morning at nine o'clock in the direction of Geneva, seven miles distant. The first three miles of road were excellent, but it began to get choppy before reaching Geneva. I was told that eight inches of snow had fallen there, with heavier falls east, which left me in a quandary as to what to do. I did not care to wait for it to dry up, as an Ohio village is not the best place to lie around, especially when everything is wet and sloppy.

A happy thought struck me as I was about to make arrangements to stop, and I was not long in putting it into operation. The Lake Shore Road [*railroad*], which runs through Geneva, is double-tracked and has a fine path between the tracks, somewhat similar to that along which Mr. Parkhurst and I had ridden out of Chicago. Very true, it was not as good as the wagon roads, but it prevented me from having to wait for the roads to dry. And besides, this was only a local storm that extended as far as Erie, Pennsylvania, some sixty miles from Geneva.

It was a dangerous undertaking, owing to the high speed of the trains as they fly along over the well-ballasted tracks. But I was willing to take the chances, passed Ashtabula and Amboy, and had dinner at Conneaut, where I met a Baptist clergyman who was on his way to Rochester, New York, on his wheel. He was about to give up riding and take the train when I came along. I asked him to dismiss the idea and accompany me. He consented and I had company once more, much to my satisfaction, as I was lonesome.

My new companion proved to be an excellent wheelman and the best of company. We were compelled to ride between the tracks all that day, however, and reached Erie, Pennsylvania, a little before dark, leaving Ohio and the snow behind us.

We had some difficulty in finding a hotel, as my companion refused to stop at one with a bar attached. After a good deal of inquiring and inconvenience, we managed to find one named the Morgan House, and I must confess that I met much nicer people there than I had previously met at hotels with gin mills attached. I would willingly have repeated the inconvenience on the rest of my journey, but I was always tired and glad to get a rest, without running around hunting up temperance hotels.

10 *On the towpath of the Erie Canal . . . And the tracks of the New York Central . . . My wheel goes home for an overhaul . . . A ride down the Hudson and a visit to Sing Sing . . . Central Park, the Battery, and the end of a wonderful ride*

The next morning we were off bright and early on our way to Buffalo, New York, ninety-seven miles from Erie. The roads had dried up sufficiently to allow us to ride over them, and we were not sorry, as the track riding had become hazardous, owing to the goodly number of fast trains in this thickly settled community. It made one feel as if his life was hanging by a thread when he propelled a bicycle on the tracks. My companion managed to have several falls that morning, which made him wish he had taken the train in place of accompanying me.

Wednesday Oct. 23

We passed out of Pennsylvania and into New York at nine o'clock, and as we crossed the line, my clergyman friend said, "The dear old state, the land of my birth!" My own dear old state was many miles behind me at that time, and I only wished that I was back there instead of where I was on that gloomy morning.

We had dinner at Fredonia, where my friend's tastes were gratified without inconvenience, as Fredonia is strictly a temperance town. He was complaining of the result of the many falls he had had that morning, however, in lieu of the whiskey tariff.

We were now forty-five miles from Buffalo, with excellent roads ahead of us, so bidding Fredonia good-bye, we rode away, passing many villages along the lake shore. We had the beautiful Lake Erie in sight until we reached Buffalo at dark.

Owing to the lateness of the hour, we dispensed with the inconvenience of looking for a temperance hotel, and besides I was not feeling well on account of eating too many of the apples for which New York State is noted. We stopped at the first hotel we came to, which proved to be the Hotel Carlton. After supper, we spent two very pleasant hours in sightseeing through the principal streets of Buffalo. We had ridden one hundred miles during the day and were ready to retire upon returning to the hotel.

Not all cyclists of the period were so casual about riding one hundred miles in a single day. In fact, awards called "century medals" were given for that very feat, and over good roads at that. On a bicycle like the Yellow Fellow, one hundred miles was a long, long way.

The following morning, October 24, dawned somewhat cold with a sharp wind blowing from the lake, reminding me that I was far from the beautiful climate of California. As we rode out Genesec Street on our way to Rochester, it was anything but comfortable. Fortunately, the roads were all that could be desired, and with the wind in our favor we went along nicely. We passed through Lancaster and Batavia, and reached Bergen in time for dinner. There are two hotels at Bergen, each supplied with a

Thursday Oct. 24

bar. This compelled my clergyman friend to dispense with his opposition, for the time being at least, in order to satisfy the inner man. He had come to the conclusion that it was the best thing to do under the circumstances, and we partook of a hearty meal.

One o'clock saw us taking our departure for our eighteen-mile ride to Rochester, where my companion was to leave me. The road still remained excellent, as is the case with all roads in this part of the state. We reached Rochester a little before three o'clock.

Rochester has quite a history. Among its many attractive resorts may be mentioned the Genesee Falls. It was here that Sam Patch—who had acquired quite a reputation before his final plunge by making an aquatic descent at Paterson, New Jersey, and by jumping into the Niagara River—met his death on the eighth of November, 1829, by plunging from the falls into the river below. Lack of space interferes with my mentioning a great many other attractions in and around Rochester.

Here my companion left me and joined his wife, who had preceded him on the train. We had become very much attached to each other, and it was with disappointment that I bade him good-bye and proceeded alone once more. This made the third companion that I had ridden with on my long journey, which made it somewhat of a common occurrence to part.

It was nearly five o'clock when I turned my back on Rochester and rode out East Avenue. The roads were very good until I reached Pittsford, but after leaving there, I had hard work wheeling through the sand until I reached Fairport. Here I concluded to ride in between the tracks of the New York Central and Hudson River Railroad, and in doing so, reached Macedon a little after dark. This village had never had more than one hotel, and that had burned down a few weeks before my arrival. This compelled me to seek accommodations at a private house occupied by a family named Karl. I was highly entertained that evening, as this was the first time a transcontinental cyclist had ever been known to stop at Macedon, and nothing was too good for me.

The following morning, October 25, saw me riding along the towpath of the Erie Canal, owing to the rugged condition of the wagon road. This did not seem to meet with the approval of the canalboat drivers, as I was continually scaring their mules. I expected to be thrown headlong into the canal every time I passed one. Here you see slow freight to your heart's content. It actually made me nervous to watch those canalboats moving along like snails. To be sure, the towpath was not the best of riding, owing to its constant use, which made it decidedly rough, but it was far better than the sand and hills through which the wagon road was built.

Friday
Oct. 25

The boatmen had the law on their side. A New York statute forbade the use of the towpath for any purpose other than driving the animals that towed the boats. The law was not well enforced, however, and Richard Wright, president of the Onandaga Historical Association, tells me that it was common for cyclists in the nineties to ride along the path. He goes on to say, "Loher was also risking arrest and a fine for trespassing on private property when he rode on the NYC &HR right-of-way. But again he was not out of line with the custom of his day." Anyway, it was a bit late in the trip for Grandfather to worry about trespassing on right-of-ways!

Occasionally, I would ride along between the tracks of the New York Central, but this was replete with danger, and I would take the towpath again at the first opportunity. I passed through Palmyra, Newark, and Lyons, and crossed the Seneca River over the New York Central bridge.

I reached Weedsport, twenty-two miles from Syracuse, at noon and had dinner at the Willard Hotel. One o'clock saw me leaving there, but within ten miles of Syracuse, the bearings ground completely out of the crankshaft of my wheel. This made it nip and tuck for me to reach Syracuse without having to walk. It was four o'clock when I reached there with my disabled wheel. I was not long in ferreting out the Stearns factory in which it was made to order another overhauling for it, so I could complete the remaining four hundred miles of my transcontinental tour.

The lobby of the Willard House, Weedsport. Grandfather stopped only for noonday dinner and so missed the pleasure of meeting the gentlemen in the lobby.
Photo courtesy: Old Brutus Historical Society.

*In view of the punishment that poor Stearns had
to take, it probably held up pretty well. Still, one has
to smile at the loyalty with which the* Syracuse Standard, *writing of Grandfather's arrival, boosted the
local product:*
    "George T. Loher *of Oakland, Cal., the trans-
continental tourist who arrived in this city Friday, is
a firm believer in the strength and stability of the
Stearns wheel, as well he may be after weighing it in
the balance of over 4,000 miles of hard usage, including hundreds of miles over the rough paths of the Rocky
mountain region. . . . Instead of proceeding due
East, [he] skirted the Pacific coast through Oregon and
Washington, thence making his way through Idaho,
Montana, the Dakotas and Minnesota to the Windy
City, from which point he has followed the beaten
paths of travel. The taking of this unusual route un-
doubtedly makes Mr. Loher's transcontinental ride the
most meritorious performance of its kind. Other cross-
continent riders have proceeded from ocean to ocean by
more direct and more easily accessible roads, but Mr.
Loher has chosen to take his way through some of the
wildest and most picturesque portions of our country,
where the roads are known only by courtesy. His arrival in New York, which is his objective point, will
signalize the close of the most important transcontinental ride yet attempted, as well as the conclusion of a
test whose rigor proves beyond the shadow of a doubt
that the Stearns is as satisfactory a mount for a journey involving thousands of miles over the roughest
country as it is for a few hours' morning spin on the
smoothest boulevards."* The writer did not find it
necessary to mention the overhaul.

The next day, Saturday, October 26, was a lonesome one for me. I hardly knew what to do to pass the time and would have willingly taken my departure, had I my wheel in riding condition. They managed to get it repaired by night, however, and the following morning, Sunday, October 27, I was on my way, accompanied by several of the boys from the factory and with almost a new wheel—so much ahead for visiting Syracuse.

We rode out Genesee Street and over the toll road to Fayetteville, eight miles distant. [*Lest the reader be confused here or think that perhaps Grandfather's notes had become scrambled, Buffalo, Syracuse, and Utica all do indeed have streets named Genesee.*] Here my escorts left me and returned to the city, while I proceeded over excellent roads to Oneida, where I had dinner at the American Hotel.

From Oneida I had the finest of roads, with bicycle path from New Hartford. This made my approach to Utica on that beautiful Sunday afternoon a most pleasant one. As I rode along Genesee Street, I was the center of attraction for the thousands of promenaders who lined the sidewalks. It was amusing to see some of them stop and watch me with their mouths wide open, as if I had just dropped from heaven or was a freak of whose identity they had not the least idea.

It was some time before sundown when I reached Utica, and I spent the time until dark riding around and viewing the city. Afterward, I registered at the Mansion House and retired early for my next day's ride through the famous Mohawk Valley.

The following morning dawned bright and clear, and I was off at half past six, riding out Albany Street. I lost my way in the hills a little south of the city, but finally managed to reach Frankfort, the first village east of Utica, where I concluded to try the towpath.

Doing so, I reached Little Falls, a beautiful little place nestled among the mountain-like hills. It reminded me very much of some of the little mountain towns which I have previously described. I was compelled to stay on the towpath after leaving Little Falls, until I reached Palatine Bridge. *Monday Oct. 28*

At Fonda, where I stopped for dinner, I was charged forty cents for a fifteen-cent meal. I presume it was for the privilege of riding through the so-called beautiful Mohawk Valley, but I failed to see the beauty. All I could see was a canyon-like valley walled in by hills, with the Mohawk River running through it. Perhaps the valley is beautiful at certain seasons of the year. It was certainly not beautiful at the time of my passing through it.

It was one o'clock when I had regained sufficient courage to continue my journey through the canyon. (It was almost an impossibility to do so on the meal I had purchased at Fonda.) A strong northwest wind enabled me to climb with ease the many hills I had to ride over.

After passing through Amsterdam, I reached Schenectady, where I came to an asphaltum pavement that had recently been sprinkled. In trying to avoid a buggy that was being driven in the opposite direction, I fell and came very near being run over. To be sure, it caused some excitement when my eager rescuers were informed that I was from California and that I had ridden all the way on my wheel. After many congratulations on my narrow escape, I continued over a sixteen-mile bicycle path and reached Albany a little before dark.

Albany's streets are very much like San Francisco's cobblestoned thoroughfares—only the ever-welcome cable slot was missing. I was compelled to bump over the cobblestones after reaching the city limits, and by the time I had reached the American Hotel, I felt as if I was experiencing a serious attack of seasickness.

Tuesday Oct. 29
The following morning I left New York's capital at half past five o'clock, crossed the Hudson River over the toll bridge, and proceeded to Castleton, south of Albany on the Hudson, for breakfast. After leaving Castleton, the hilly condition of the country made my ride down the Hudson anything but pleasant.

I finally reached the village of Hudson, with the Catskill Mountains (made famous by Rip Van Winkle) on the opposite bank. The scenery along here is beautiful and romantic. Who has not seen or read of the famous Hudson River scenery, excelled by none and only rivaled by the beautiful Rhine, which Germany never ceases to praise?

After leaving Hudson village, I see many beautiful mansions along the river banks in endless variety of architecture. How particular the occupants are in placing inscriptions, such as "Keep Out," "No Trespassing," and so on, as if they wanted to be alone with their hoarded gold and magnificent surroundings! There are kind-hearted people among them, however, who allow people the privilege of walking through the grounds and admiring the beauties of nature, but they are few and far between.

I reached Red Hook for dinner and was overcharged again for a scant meal. I must confess the accommodations were most contemptible along the Hudson. I really believe I would have suffered from hunger, had it not been for the deliciously flavored apples that I found so abundant at the farms along its banks. After leaving Red Hook, I passed through Rhinecliff, one of the prettiest and most aristocratic villages on the Hudson. It is here that most of the millionaires and rich bankers live.

Poughkeepsie, the largest city between Albany and New York, was my next stopping place. A foolhardy adventurer looking for notoriety had jumped from the Lake Shore Railroad's high bridge only a few days before my arrival there and was killed. My stay in Poughkeepsie was of short duration, the high bridge being the only attraction. After I had viewed it, I proceeded on my journey.

Fishkill is the next principal village. Here the historic Newburgh [*George Washington's headquarters in 1782–83*] can be seen on the opposite side of the river. It was nearly sundown when I reached there, so I decided to keep on and stop at Cold Springs, ten miles south, for the night.

My travels now were replete with beautiful scenery and good roads. On arising the following morning, October 30, a splendid view of the Palisades and West Point met my gaze as I looked out of my window at the hotel. This, coupled with the thoughts of being close to the end of my trip, made it a pleasant morning for me. *Wednesday Oct. 30*

Shortly after seven o'clock I bid Cold Springs goodbye and left for my fifty-two-mile ride to New York City. The roads for the first ten miles were miserable and reminded me very much of the Montana country. But the thoughts of being so close to the end of my journey gave me encouragement, and I overcame the inconveniences and reached Peekskill, the great stove manufacturing city, at nine o'clock.

From Peekskill to Sing Sing, the roads were a little better, but nothing to brag of. Upon arriving at Sing

Sing, I decided to visit the prison. In doing so, I saw Dr. Meyer, the infamous poisoner, and McKane, the Coney Island boodler, together with a host of other celebrities too numerous to mention.

Intrigued by Grandfather's rather cryptic description of these two gentlemen, no doubt familiar names on front pages of the time, I did some historical detective work in a microfilm file of the New York Times.

McKane seems to have been a Watergate plumber of his day. He was sentenced in 1894 to serve six years for inducing election inspectors to conceal registry lists, making it possible to cast many fraudulent votes. A number of officials were involved in the conspiracy.

The tollgate at Fayetteville, New York. Not all the toll roads Grandfather encountered on the trip were as legitimate as this one.

Photo courtesy: Onondaga Historical Society.

Grandfather rode in via Central Park. "As it was a summerlike afternoon, the wealthy people were out for an airing. Some were in handsome barouches."
Photo courtesy: New York Historical Society.

Dr. Henry C. W. Meyer had more imagination. In fact, detectives who had been on his trail for years claimed that half his criminal acts would never be known. It seems that Dr. Meyer was given to insuring people's lives, then killing them and collecting on the policies. He had been tried twice in Chicago for having poisoned his first wife and his son in such a scheme, but he was acquitted both times.

While in jail on the second occasion, he met Gustav Baum, a fellow prisoner charged with forgery. After their release, Meyer returned to his medical practice, and Baum became his collector. Together they hatched a new plot. Baum was to take out insurance policies with four companies for a total of $8,500, after which he would feign severe illness. They would then find a body, pass it off as a just-deceased Baum, and divide the insurance money between them. Mrs. Meyer (a fearless woman, we may be sure!) posed as Baum's wife so that when he "died" she could collect *the insurance without arousing suspicion.*

That was the plan proposed to Baum. After the policies were issued, however, Dr. Meyer and his wife began slipping their partner small doses of arsenic. It caused a chronic dysentery, and Baum grew weaker and weaker. He must have been an uncommonly trusting man, for he remained in the care of Dr. Meyer until he died, in March of 1892.

Two of the insurance companies paid "Mrs. Baum" without question. A third noticed that she was in rather a hurry to collect the benefits and decided to investigate. The Meyers fled but were eventually arrested in Detroit and brought to New York for trial.

The trial must have been something of a circus. The first day, of 160 prospective jurors all but six were dismissed. Eventually proceedings got underway, but on the last day of the trial, while the defense was summing up, one of the jurors went berserk, and the entire case had to be tried again.

Warden Sage kindly allowed me to visit the execution chamber, a privilege very rarely allowed anyone. The guard invited me to sit in the electrical chair. I did so and found it a comfortable piece of furniture (that is, when the dynamo is not running) notwithstanding that it has been the means of ending the existence of several individuals. I was shown the different attachments that go to complete the execution of the condemned. I was also told that three or four men and a woman were waiting to be legally done to death.

After bidding the warden good-bye, I departed from Sing Sing and reached Tarrytown in time for dinner, after which I passed through Yonkers. Here I could see Harlem with its high bridges in the distance.

Soon after leaving Yonkers, I met a wheelman going in the direction of New York. He kindly showed me to the limits of the great city, after which I rode down Seventh Avenue until I entered Central Park, a little after three.

As it was a summerlike afternoon, the wealthy people were out for an airing. Some were in handsome barouches, others on horseback, while others were riding bicycles. As I rode through with my odd-looking uniform and dusty appearance, they would gaze at me in amazement, wondering what freak had been let loose now.

I had shunned all newspaper reporters long before reaching New York, as they had become a source of annoyance to me. In fact, I became perfectly tired of relating the same story over and over. Consequently, I rode into New York unknown to anyone save a few friends, and they were unaware of the exact date of my arrival.

My ride through the park was a very pleasant one. The many things to be seen there, especially the vast number of different-styled vehicles, made it most interesting for me. I rode out of it at Fifty-ninth Street and Fifth Avenue, where the numerous first-class hotels, such as the Savoy, the Netherlands, and others are situated.

My ride on Fifth Avenue cobblestones was of short duration, however, as I was not in need of a shaking up. I turned to my right until I reached Eighth Avenue, where I came on to an asphaltum pavement, and reached the Battery, after dodging around the numerous teams so essential on New York's downtown thoroughfares.

This completed my transcontinental bicycle tour of 4,354 miles from San Francisco to New York City. I had

*Boating on the lake in Central Park the year before Grandfather's ride. Did he court Grand-
mother here in this romantic setting? I guess we'll never know.*
Photo courtesy: New York Historical Society.

left San Francisco [*actually Oakland*] on Sunday, August
11, and half past four o'clock, Wednesday afternoon, October 30, saw me at the Battery in New York City. I was
exactly eighty days in completing the trip, sixty-three of
which were consumed by actual riding.

Now let me conclude my experiences by saying that if
you ever cross the continent on a bicycle, I sincerely hope
you will meet with better roads, more congenial people,
and last but not least, a stronger bicycle than I had.

The End.

Epilogue

In spite of all that he had already seen and experienced, Grandfather was a wide-eyed tourist in New York City. He tells us a little of his five-week stay in these paragraphs at the end of his journal:

During my stay in New York, I was a guest of the New Manhattan Club, one of the largest and finest in the United States.

I visited Ellis Island, where the dreamers of Europe are examined before being allowed to land on our beautiful shores. Two Italian ships had unloaded 964 immigrants the day I visited the island, and it was disgusting to see the inspectors maul those poor unfortunates around as if they were cattle.

I also visited the Eden Muse [*Musée*], the Bowery, and the Brooklyn Bridge. It is useless to endeavor to tell all I saw in New York during my five weeks' stay there.

I will say in conclusion, if you are a Californian and have not seen the great and wicked city of New York, do not fail to grasp the first opportunity of doing so. Germany has her Berlin, France her Paris, Russia her St. Petersburg, but the United States can boast of having only one real cosmopolitan city, and that one is New York. You can see low life and high life, and when you're through, you will wonder how it is that one half of the world does not know how the other half lives.

But there was one significant event that, curiously, Grandfather doesn't even mention. While in New York, he met a young lady, actually a third cousin, named Ellen Riley. He must have seemed to her dashing indeed, still in the flush of his cross-country triumph. And he must have been equally smitten by this demure flower he found there in the "wicked" city, for they were married in Oakland in November of the following year.

* * *

On December 14, 1895, the San Francisco Call *carried a brief item:*

LOHER RETURNS.

Rode His Bicycle Across the Continent.

George Loher, who went East several months ego on a bicycle, returned on the overland to-day. He rode through to New York city, but was satisfied to return by train. He will resume his place in Becker's market Monday.